A Year of Self-Compassion

A Year of Self-Compassion

Finding care, connection
and calm in our challenging times.

AMANDA SUPER

Matador
9 Priory Business Park,
Wistow Road, Kibworth Beauchamp,
Leicestershire. LE8 0RX
Tel: 0116 279 2299
Email: books@troubador.co.uk
Web: www.troubador.co.uk/matador
Twitter: @matadorbooks

ISBN 978 1784624 255

British Library Cataloguing in Publication Data.
A catalogue record for this book is available from the British Library.

Printed and bound by CPI Group (UK) Ltd, Croydon, CR0 4YY
Typeset in 10.5pt AldineBT by Troubador Publishing Ltd, Leicester, UK

Matador is an imprint of Troubador Publishing Ltd

For Millie and Monty – may your lives be filled with compassion for yourselves and others.

CONTENTS

INTRODUCTION

Self-compassion is a relatively new field although it has been studied academically for the last ten years or so. The research and data produced so far has shown how beneficial self-compassion can be in regard to our health and well-being and how it significantly improves our relationship with ourselves and, in turn, those around us. Developing self-compassion can enable us to increase our resilience to manage the inevitable challenges of life – both the significant such as bereavement, illness, divorce/separation, financial worries, stressful situations and the less profound, such as daily frustrations like traffic, technological difficulties and running out of milk!

By developing self-compassion we can not only learn to deal with challenges but also learn to thrive when life is less testing. Self-compassion enables us to develop self-acceptance, which research shows improves our health and well-being and deepens our sense of life satisfaction, even if our circumstances haven't significantly changed.

Another great benefit to developing self-compassion is that it is entirely self-supporting, in that we don't need anything or anyone other than ourselves to help us practice the fundamental aspects. Furthermore, self-compassion can be learnt and this is what will you will be introduced to during the course of this journal. We can start the journey towards self-compassion from exactly where we are, in fact, at any time, in any place, anywhere will do.

This reflective journal has been created to enable you to build compassion for yourself and others. It is based upon the latest research and most up to date knowledge in the field of self-development related to the subject of compassion and mindfulness.

Amanda Super is a chartered psychologist and coach with over twenty years of experience in the field of personal and professional development. She has brought her expertise to the subject of compassion as a means of developing our understanding and practice of this cutting edge phenomenon. This work is based on her own journey towards developing self-compassion and the journeys of the many clients Amanda has provided psychological interventions to over the course of her career.

It is understood that true compassion starts with the self. In Western culture we can view ourselves in a way that often actually undermines our ability to see ourselves clearly – as human beings doing the best we can and, for the most part, not just surviving, but succeeding. We have very high expectations of how we should be and perform in every area of our lives. If we don't meet these aspirations we can tend to view ourselves as failing in some way. We often only fail to see all that we actually are – exactly as we are, not perfect, but mostly good enough.

Self-compassion provides us with a tool to authentically develop our self-acceptance, self-worth and self-esteem in a way that allows us to be caring and considerate towards both ourselves and others without being dependent on outside factors. As the Dalai Lama pointed out, "We don't have to earn the right to compassion; it is our birthright."

This reflective journal will take you on an engaging journey towards self-compassion by considering its three main components and allowing you to apply these concepts in relation to yourself and your life. These three key elements are:

• Being caring towards ourselves
• Recognising our connection to others
• Learning to be mindful in the moment

It takes courage to accept ourselves as we are, but with guidance and support we can embrace the opportunity to consider ourselves and our lives differently. Taking inspiration from some of the most acclaimed thinkers of our time and offering reflections on their ideas about compassion and all it encompasses, Amanda has developed this reflective journal. Through her encouraging and reassuring, as well as practical suggestions, you will be guided towards a deeper, more meaningful and understanding approach towards the challenges of life. A life of greater care, connection and calm awaits you, empowering you to think, feel and act more compassionately towards yourself and in turn, others.

HOW TO USE THIS
REFLECTIVE JOURNAL

Self-development can be greater and have more longevity when we actively engage with a subject, whilst we document and chart its course in our lives. Over the coming year, to write each week about the chosen reflection and its meaning to you will offer you the chance to gain clarity and track your progress on an ongoing basis. Completing the weekly journal pages will allow you the opportunity for deeper and more meaningful reflection considering how you think, feel and may act when bearing the reflections presented in mind.

This idea is based on the cognitive behavioural psychotherapeutic tradition which encourages us to identify our thoughts as they lead us to the feelings we experience which in turn form the basis of our behaviours. At first, separating out what we think and working out what emotion we feel can be challenging. At times, we all struggle to identify our feelings. A list of possible emotions is provided in the Further Resources section to assist you with this. With practice, recognising our thoughts and feelings does come more easily, try to be kind and patient with yourself as more is revealed whilst you progress along your journey towards experiencing greater self-compassion.

To acknowledge the aspects of our lives for which we are grateful is a well observed psychological method to develop our happiness and appreciation for all that is good in our lives, as well as our levels of self-acceptance. You are therefore encouraged to consider at least one aspect of your life for which you are grateful each week when completing the journal pages. The expression of gratitude in our lives has been found to have a hugely beneficial psychological impact on our well-being. Developing this skill helps us to view our lives in greater balance by bringing us deeper insight and appreciation for all that we have.

There are a number of ways you can use this journal to suit your needs. However, from the research we have conducted, we would suggest that you read the reflections, one at a time, in the order they are presented, perhaps on a set day each week and then complete the accompanying journal page to the best of your ability. We have found that by setting a day of the week where you know you are likely to be able to find ten minutes where you can read the reflection in full, followed by filling in your journal responses, can set you up to practice aspects of self-compassion during the week ahead. You may then want to refer back to the reflection and your writing at various points during the week and add any further points that are relevant to you and your life. You can also just dip in and out of the various subjects presented depending on what you would find helpful at any given time.

You are encouraged to find inspiration from this reflective journal in any way that feels useful to you. Feel free to complete the learning review provided every four weeks to help you evaluate your progress. You may find it helpful to colour in the patterns provided as a source of mindful relaxation.

It is our sincere hope that the journal YOU create, based on the many wise and wonderful insights presented, will empower you towards a life more full of compassion, a deeper sense of peace, greater happiness and a stronger sense of self-supporting well-being.

THE THREE

COMPONENTS OF

SELF-COMPASSION

EXPLAINED

COMPONENT ONE – BEING CARING TOWARDS OURSELVES

Self-Kindness

The first core component of self-compassion involves developing self-kindness. This consists of learning to respond in a warm and caring way towards ourselves when we find ourselves struggling in some way. We as human beings, albeit at different times and in various ways, will inevitably experience a variety of perfectly reasonable fears and concerns. These may be in relation to our working lives and careers, our relationships with others, our financial security, our health or the well-being and safety of those we care for, or a general anxiety about the world we live in. There are also times where we can feel inadequate in some way, make mistakes, fail to reach a goal or are just unsure of ourselves or a situation we are in. At times, we may feel hurt by someone's behaviour towards us or feel let down by others we thought we could depend upon. Developing self-kindness helps us to stop criticising ourselves for feeling the way we do, instead we are able to offer ourselves a kind and understanding response, akin to the sort of response we might give to the people we care for, if they were experiencing similar worries or difficulties.

To learn to act towards ourselves with understanding and to silence the critical voice in our heads that can sometimes appear are the first steps towards living a more compassionate life. Furthermore, we need to find ways to respond to our challenges with soothing comfort when life feels difficult. If we can offer empathy towards ourselves, we are not letting ourselves off the hook, but recognising that we are only human. We will inevitably make mistakes or fail to live up to our expectations. We can learn and grow from these, rather than criticise ourselves endlessly about how we must do better or how we are to blame. We often grow more as human beings as a result of the difficulties we experience rather than the easy times. So even though it doesn't feel like it at the time, to be kind to ourselves when life is difficult, to ask ourselves what do we need right now and to acknowledge the pain we are in, allows the healing process to begin.

When we can give ourselves kindness and acceptance, we feel less need to have others provide it for us. We can become more self-supporting in a way that is sustainable and not reliant on anyone or anything outside of ourselves to make us feel better. We are all capable of self-care as we are evolutionarily designed to give this to our offspring, and we can therefore learn to allow the same innate mechanism to provide comfort and support towards ourselves when we need it. We can learn to see ourselves as valuable and worthy of care. We can feel more secure as we respond to our difficulties, knowing that we can always offer ourselves a place of safety to recover and heal. We can learn to experience this love and compassion from within by developing the habit of self-kindness.

Appreciating Ourselves

Developing self-appreciation can allow us to recognise our positive qualities and strengths. We are often fearful that to feel any such appreciation might appear as if we are arrogant. It is clear however, that acknowledging our accomplishments and abilities is no more self-centred than having compassion for our weaknesses.

If we struggle with our self-regard, we usually adopt various defence mechanisms to try to protect ourselves from the hurt we might feel if someone else fails to appreciate us. By developing self-compassion we become less susceptible to other's views of us and have less need to protect or defend ourselves as we know we aren't perfect, whilst recognising that neither is anyone else. The trick here is to avoid making any comparisons of ourselves to others as this only serves to undermine our self-worth. The reality is that we are no better or worse than anyone else, we are all equally amazing, as well as flawed, just by virtue of being human. We can learn to truly value what we bring to the world by practising small and quiet acts of self-appreciation.

In our responses to others recognising our worth, we can start to accept a compliment with a simple 'thank you', rather than dismissal or a self-inflicted personal put down that diminishes their appreciation of us and undermines our own sense of worth. For example, a colleague tells you that they thought you performed a particular task well and your response might be either dismissive such as, "Oh that, it was nothing," or open criticism of yourself, such as, "Oh that, I thought it was rubbish." Changing these small but significant behaviours can enable us to start to believe that we are worthy of appreciation and we do have many positive qualities and abilities, whilst recognising that as human beings we will never be perfect.

Cultivating self-appreciation in our day to day lives is an extension of developing self-compassion at more challenging times. They are different sides of the same coin. Self-esteem is different from self-compassion in that it is highly dependent on external factors based on the idea that we need to be special or above average to feel good about ourselves. So efforts to raise self-esteem can result in self-absorbed behaviour and require us to put other people down to feel ok. We can move beyond aiming for self-esteem to giving ourselves the acceptance, approval and praise that we need regardless of who we are and where we are in life.

Developing self-compassion allows us to form a positive inner dialogue that affirms us and leaves us less susceptible to the views of others. We no longer need to expose our vulnerabilities by making comparisons of ourselves to other people. We can, in fact, start to show appreciation for the strengths and abilities of others without feeling as if that belittles us in any way. By accepting ourselves for who we are, no better or worse than anyone else, neither perfect nor beyond help, in a quiet and meaningful way, we can alter the way we appreciate ourselves and all that we have to offer. We can move beyond the need to judge ourselves and, in turn, others. We are all unique. Equally, we are all works in progress.

By developing a greater sense of self-appreciation and self-kindness we are naturally building resilience against the challenges that life will inevitably throw our way, as well as recognising, with a sense of gratitude, all that is good in us and in our lives. The best part of all is that we can start this process anytime, from exactly where we are, right now.

Cultural Influences

In Western culture, we are almost programmed to continually achieve and can feel less than adequate if we fail to do so consistently. Many of us are also culturally taught to judge ourselves and others harshly. We cannot underestimate the power of the social norms we experience on a daily basis, both the obvious and the more subtle.

The culture we live in seems to place much of its value on various aspects of fame and fortune. This is coupled with a need to celebrate the inevitable 'downfall' of those we seemingly revere to the point of actually finding enjoyment in their unhappiness. This takes the form of the multitude of reality TV shows that purposefully engage people in insulting or derogatory tasks or look for any opportunity to cause them embarrassment or shame, as well as the more well established methods that post endless unflattering pictures online or in print. Our culture suggests that we should feel pressure to try to emulate the people who are celebrated, in the way we look and dress or the lifestyle we are able to afford and maintain. We are taught to revere money and all it can bring us. Unfortunately fame and fortune offer no guarantee of good health and happiness – the two things that, as human beings, we all struggle without.

We are at a point in our history where if you were to ask many Western children what they would like to achieve in life, it would be likely that they aspire to be 'rich and famous' in some way. As a society, we think these things will bring us unlimited happiness and the approval of our peers. Children are very intuitive and recognise what they see as being successful – be it rounds of applause on a talent show or football pitch or pictures of unusually beautiful people in magazines. Our culture reveres these things and children therefore naturally aspire to them.

We as adults can aspire to similar narratives; in fact the Western world is built on the ideas of success we have culturally formed. It is no wonder then that many of us feel we are lacking in some way if we are not achieving such 'success' on a daily basis. We expect the unattainable and don't believe we will be happy until we achieve these misplaced goals to perfection. How could we do it any differently when these are the goals our society sets for us? How can we start to value finding the extraordinary in the ordinary humdrum of daily life? The regular tasks many of us find ourselves engaged in can seem pretty boring for the most part – laundry, cooking, food shopping, working, driving, cleaning, the list is endless! How can we feel that we are enough, exactly as we are in this very moment and happy and satisfied with our lot, without feeling the driving need to glorify the busy and achieve (mostly silent) applause for all that we do daily, including how we present ourselves to the world?

One of the answers is to learn to practice to treat ourselves with kindness, compassion and self-acceptance for who we are and where we are right now. To reduce our expectations of both ourselves and the things that constitute success in our culture, as these are generally a privilege many around the world are never likely to see. When we always aspire to more and kid ourselves that we will be happy when certain things comes to fruition, we will always be chasing an elusive pot of gold at the end of the rainbow which, for the most part, does not exist and probably would not make us truly happy anyway!

We can never attain true perfection in ourselves or our lives, and no amount of trying can probably change this. We still need to do what we can to the best of our ability – work hard, play fair, act and behave with integrity, give of ourselves to those in need and fulfil our responsibilities. However, for the most part, we *are* good enough and likely to be very fortunate in many ways. By acknowledging this and truly accepting it, through regularly reminding ourselves of such facts, we can and will feel a greater sense of peace and deeper satisfaction with the reality of our lives as they are, right here and right now.

Looking After the Basics

To value ourselves we need to also practice daily rituals that show care and respect for our bodies, as well as our minds and spirit. By eating a healthy diet, exercising in ways we actually enjoy, drinking enough water to sustain our bodily functions, sleeping enough each night and taking time out to relax all contribute to our feelings of well-being. By looking after these basic physical needs we will inevitably feel stronger, better in ourselves and healthier. These actions constitute a form of self-kindness and positive self-regard. Many of us are able to recognise the need to provide this focus to maintain healthy living regarding the lives of our children, and we need to learn to apply the same logic to ourselves.

To look after our minds we need to engage in activities that bring us happiness and a sense of achievement, even in small ways. Going for a walk in a natural setting or having a long hot bath can be relaxing experiences that allow the senses to absorb the environment, as well as allowing us space and time to just be, rather than do. Activities that engage the mind creatively such as baking a cake, doing a crossword, knitting a scarf, colouring a picture, reading a book or gardening can all provide us with opportunites to escape the ordinary and feel a sense of accomplishment. Activities that engage the body can assist too, such as going for a run or a bike ride, dancing, going to an exercise class or the gym or being involved in a team sport. If we can make the time to give something back to our communities in the form of voluntary work, the rewards can be amazing. Finding purposeful ways to engage our minds and bodies can help us avoid both boredom and complacency as well as allowing us to recognise that it is in the achievement of small but expressive tasks that we can feel a deeper sense of meaning in our lives and a quiet satisfaction.

Facing the Challenges

Life throws many challenges at us, regardless of our status and standing in society. One of the biggest obstacles to showing resilience and coping with the difficulties is in the way we talk to ourselves. Our thinking about ourselves and our ability to cope can be the difference between getting through a hard patch or allowing it to define us and who we think we are. Thinking of ourselves in negative terms can undermine our ability to manage whilst trying to keep our self-respect and dignity intact. When we recognise that we are resourceful human beings that can manage adversity well and not berate ourselves for finding things tough, we have a better chance of getting through the inevitable difficulties.

We need to form new expressions of how we think and how we speak to ourselves. A positive and compassionate focus is helpful here. In moments of challenge, to have a statement that we can silently say to ourselves that supports us, recognises the difficulty and responds with kindness can make all the difference to how we feel about and how we face the obstacles in our path. There are suggestions for self-compassion statements in the Further Resources section of this journal. Although it must be acknowledged that no saying will remove the difficulty, even a slight change in our perception, which silently repeating a statement can bring about, can make all the difference to how we cope with the challenges we have to face.

When there are no significant challenges before us and we feel generally that everything is ok with our world, we can still benefit from cultivating a deeper sense of self-acceptance. By recognising our strengths and the things we do well and reminding ourselves of our achievements can be life affirming and empowering. We can all try to acknowledge three things that we have done well each week. We can also think of something that might have gone better, but it's important not to dwell on this for too long. Just recognise and acknowledge it but look for the learning this experience offers. By appreciating the good things we bring to the world, just by being ourselves, a stronger sense of who we are and what our purpose is can take root.

By focusing on sowing the seeds of self-compassion and practising small acts of self-kindness, in good times and bad, we can transform the lives we live. This journal will encourage you to develop these habits so that they become just part of the way we live and function on a daily basis. Every moment offers an opportunity for renewal and we can begin again, whenever we choose, to embrace a kinder and more compassionate way to relate to and treat ourselves.

COMPONENT TWO – CONNECTING WITH OTHERS

We Are Never Alone

The second core component of self-compassion is the recognition that we are all in this together and we, as human beings, share a common human experience. The frustration we can feel when things go wrong, or when certain aspects of our lives aren't exactly as we want them to be, is often accompanied by a strong sense of isolation. It can feel as if we are the only ones to have ever felt the way we do, be going through these situations, experiencing these disappointments or having these concerns. In truth, all humans suffer – we are all fallible, vulnerable and imperfect.

Self-compassion allows us to recognise that suffering is part of the shared human experience – something we all go through, not something that happens to us alone. The reality is that there is nothing that any of us experience that another person hasn't experienced before. We are all interconnected as a human race in this way. There is no one on the planet who doesn't experience some form of difficulty between the time of their birth and death. Not one of us is immune to the suffering that sometimes accompanies living in the world and the challenges that face us, although it is critical to acknowledge that some suffer a great deal more than others.

In all likelihood, most of us will experience some form of challenge on a fairly regular basis – this is what it is to live. That is the case for all of us, although all difficulties are relative to the time and place we find ourselves living in. Self-compassion allows us to recognise that we are all just doing our best with the cards we have been dealt, and every single human being on the planet just wants to be happy and thrive, regardless of the circumstances they find themselves in.

Self-compassion enables us to recognise that everyone suffers. Feelings of inadequacy and disappointment are shared by all of us, albeit at different times, in different circumstances and to varying degrees. The process is the same and our acknowledgement of this can actually provide us with some comfort because it allows us to see how much we have in common with our fellow travellers on this journey called life, and how, even though it might feel like it at times, we are never alone.

The Reality of Life

By accepting the fact that life is difficult, ironically, it can actually become much easier. As opposed to always expecting things to go well or to feel happy in every moment, we can better anticipate the reality that we are likely to encounter challenges along the way. Always chasing the positive aspects of life doesn't give us the opportunity to benefit from the difficulties in the ways we might. It also doesn't prepare us for or increase our resilience in the face of adversity.

Developing self-compassion can help to reduce our expectation that life will always be plain sailing. It is inevitable that at times we will fail. We will experience hardship in a myriad of ways. We will feel hurt by another's behaviour towards us. We will feel alone and uncertain. We will struggle with our overwhelming responsibilities. We will lose people we care for and experience health difficulties or illnesses, both in ourselves and our loved ones. At times, there is no getting away from the fact that life is just hard. A sense of isolation from others can make life feel harder still.

The reality is that we are all card-carrying members of the human race, in the same boat when it comes to negotiating the challenges of life, therefore none of us are truly alone in this regard. There is no difficulty that comes along that another person hasn't experienced, even if we don't know them personally. Sometimes this realisation can really support and comfort us in times of need as it taps into our sense of common humanity and responds to our biological need to belong and connect with others. We never need to feel isolated again, even if we are physically alone, when we can appreciate all the similarities we share with our fellow human beings.

Realistic Expectations

Our expectations can lead us to a lifetime of disappointment. The amount we expect of ourselves and whether we see ourselves as perfect and/or successful can have a huge impact on our health and well-being. The reality is that we will never reach perfection – in any area of our lives. It is unrealistic and exhausting to put this constant pressure on ourselves. It is more likely that we will achieve many of our aims and objectives in life by just doing the next right thing and trying our best, knowing that we are doing all we can and that this effort is good enough. Sometimes it is helpful for us to question why we are striving for certain things; are these truly for our own benefit or to gain the approval and admiration of others? When we focus on bettering ourselves and our lives, looking through the lens of self-compassion can help to keep our expectations truly focused on what is really important to us.

We can also expect too little from ourselves at times. We might consider certain options and choices are out of the question for us because we don't have the self-belief or confidence in ourselves to have a go. Self-compassion can encourage us to try, even if we don't end up where we might have hoped, and allows us to see what we have gained and learnt from the experience. Fear can hold us back, even if we aren't fully aware of what it is we are frightened of. By developing self-compassion we are giving ourselves a chance to view ourselves and our lives differently, more accurately, in that we can see ourselves as doing the best we can with what we have got. We underestimate how much benefit we can get from trying new things, even when they feel scary and unfamiliar. We are capable of learning to approach things differently and if we make a mistake or get things wrong, we can see that this often isn't the end of the world and others don't think any less of us. However, it is our view of ourselves that is more important here, in valuing ourselves and recognising how we tried, regardless of others' views.

The expectations of our families, our partners, our friends, our teachers, our bosses and any number of other people can either put so much pressure on us that we start to fail to meet their expectations or it can drive us forward. We need both the support and challenge of others, one of these alone is not enough to succeed in any meaningful way that can be sustained. When we have people around us who clearly show that they believe in us and all we can achieve, this can assist us even way beyond our own hopes and dreams.

We are not always blessed with people who understand what support and challenge we might benefit from. Often the expectations we have of others can also lead to a huge amount of heartache and distress as they are unable to recognise our need for unconditional positive regard or are just unable to provide it. Many people cannot, for whatever reason, meet their own needs, let alone ours! When we expect others to meet our needs and they fail to do so, we can feel hugely let down. By developing self-compassion, we become less reliant on others to provide us with approval or recognition, as we become more able to give this support to ourselves.

Recognition of our common humanity allows us to reduce our expectations of ourselves and those around us. We don't have much power to influence the expectations others have of us other than to point out that we are living our lives as we see fit and their expectations are exactly that – theirs! Trying to cultivate honest and open communication with others starts with being self-aware and understanding ourselves better. What we want and need, only we ourselves can decide. To be able to communicate these needs, either directly or indirectly, with those around us can empower us to follow our own path in life. This is the start of knowing and recognising our boundaries, and then the work really begins when we do all we can to maintain them! Through developing self-compassion, we can learn to understand our needs and practise communicating them.

Making Comparisons

Often it is in our comparison of ourselves to others, both known and unknown to us, which can cause us additional and unnecessary suffering. When we are struggling we can feel we are acutely different from others, and this is only exacerbated when we compare ourselves or our situations to those of other people. Whether we think we are better off than others or worse off in some way, this approach only heightens our sense of isolation. It deepens our sense of dissatisfaction with ourselves and our lives and encourages us to feel more disconnected and different.

Having compassion for ourselves allows us to recognise we are good enough as we are and for where we are in life. We no longer need to put other people down to feel better about ourselves or exaggerate aspects of our own lives. Every one of us is valuable, exactly as we are, neither better or worse than anyone else, more or less successful than others and, most importantly, not significantly different from anyone else. We all have our own unique gifts and abilities to bring to the world.

Developing self-compassion allows us to be glad for others when they achieve their aspirations, and these in no way belittle or demean our own achievements. We are all on our own journeys. We don't need to be perfect or strive for perfection. We do not need to be dependent on the approval or validation of others; by developing self-compassion we can learn to give this to ourselves. We become free to be all that we are and we can actually thrive rather than endlessly strive.

We find ourselves in this life through no choice of our own. Some of the struggles we experience are based on our inability to accept our failings, whether we are responsible for them or not. Whilst as adults we are responsible for ourselves, we need to acknowledge that many of our thoughts, feelings and behaviours are influenced by external factors such as our genes, upbringing and role models as well as the culture we live in and the actions and expectations of others. Most of our features, and therefore some of the circumstances of our lives, are not entirely of our choosing, other outside influences play a part. On this basis, we are essentially interdependent as many of our experiences are impacted upon by elements we have no control over. To accept and acknowledge this we become more able to take it less personally when things go awry. We are better able to see the challenges with understanding and non-judgemental compassion and to tap into our common humanity.

Human beings have a deep need to bond and form connections. By recognising our inherent interconnectedness to others, coupled with our biological need to belong, we can feel less isolated and accept ourselves more fully and the situations we find ourselves in. When we can be true to ourselves and feel real compassion towards ourselves and others, we inevitably enhance our sense that we are a worthwhile part of the human race. When we focus on our similarities, rather than our differences to each other, we can offer genuine empathy and compassion to our fellow travellers, as well as to ourselves. We don't need to compare ourselves to others or equate our value with our perceptions of other people. We all just want to belong and feel accepted, and we all want to succeed and be happy as much as the next person. To have compassion allows us to be glad for another's achievements which in turn can lead us towards greater opportunities for our own happiness.

We are all connected as human beings but we are not responsible for other adults and nor are they responsible for us. Just as we don't always get things right, neither will they. Others are just not able to meet all our needs. We need to be as self-supporting as possible, knowing all the while that we are not alone and there are many other people around the world experiencing similar things to us, even if we don't know them. The human condition is exactly that, a human experience and none of us are immune to the twists and turns of life.

Our being human is always with us; it never leaves. We are all imperfect human beings doing the best we can and therefore we are all connected in this way as members of the human race. If we were perfect, we wouldn't be human! We all experience the wonder and amazement of life as well as the sorrows and fears. We find ourselves in this life through no choice of our own. We have to accept where we have come from and that we all have strengths as well as areas that could be developed. But that is what makes us human and we all have this common bond throughout our lives. Using this journal will develop your ability to become more self-supporting whilst helping you to recognise your interdependence in relation to others. It will also act as a reminder of the fact that you are never alone, knowing that you share your journey with countless others. By respecting and honouring our humanity, we are more able to feel compassion for ourselves and all our fellow human beings as we negotiate the experience of life.

COMPONENT THREE – BEING MINDFUL IN THE MOMENT

The Science of Mindfulness

There is a growing body of research evidence to suggest that the practice of mindfulness can have a significant effect on our health and well-being. Emerging knowledge confirms what has been 'known' for centuries within Eastern philosophy and traditions, that mindfulness is extremely beneficial in its ability to soothe and comfort the human mind.

Mindfulness is now being used and taught to target various forms of physical and mental health issues with strong evidence to support the success of such interventions. As human beings, each and every one of us, by definition, has physical and mental health. We do not need a formal diagnosis of any sort to feel the benefit the practice of mindfulness can bring. At its most basic level, the development of a mindful approach increases our ability to cope with life's challenges, and as we have already recognised, none of us are immune to these.

Noticing Without Judgement

To be mindful simply means that we are aware of how we are thinking, feeling and behaving in the present moment without judging ourselves. We neither supress nor exaggerate our emotions but are able to hold them in mindful awareness. When we are able to pay attention to the present moment, in a mindful way, we will have greater emotional balance. Reality dictates that we cannot ignore our pain and feel compassion for it at the same time. Mindfulness allows us to become aware of what is going on in the moment and encourages us to find a compassionate response.

There are many ways we can try to see ourselves more clearly, without judgement, including focusing on our breathing, meditating, writing or even just taking a moment to notice how we feel and allowing space for this awareness to surface. The key here is noticing, not judging or trying to change or fix how we think or feel, just noticing with compassionate awareness. This allows us to be less caught up in the actual thoughts and emotions and, rather than get swept away by them, find ourselves able to hold them more calmly than we would probably do otherwise.

The practice of mindfulness gives us the space we need before we launch into reacting, often projecting our fears and hurt towards others. We can become less reactive in regard to what is going on around us by exercising mindfulness. We can develop our ability to reflect and understand ourselves more fully, give ourselves the kindness we need and recognise our common humanity so that our responses to our difficulties are more mindful as well as measured.

Avoiding the Pain of Life

Life is painful, this is an indisputable fact. Emotional suffering is often based on us wanting our lives to be different in some way. But, pain is part of life; disappointment, failure to reach our goals and ideals, the loss of people, places and things are all part of the rich tapestry of life. Difficulties and challenges will inevitably arise. Others' behaviour and actions will, at times, cause us pain. Equally, we will not get things right every time. We will make mistakes, hurt other people and ourselves, mostly unintentionally as well as make our fair share of poor choices. To practise mindfulness is to hold our emotional responses in our conscious awareness, which can actually lessen our suffering. By learning to accept ourselves, it doesn't let us off the hook or give us permission to behave how we like with no thought as to the consequences of our actions, but reminds us to be vigilant and use these experiences to increase our awareness of ourselves to learn and grow as people.

It is important to remember that not all the thoughts and feelings we have are of our own choosing. Psychological theory has, for decades, understood that many of our current behaviours are based on the things we needed to do to survive in an earlier part of our lives. Issues we have may stem from having felt different to others, from being scared or uncertain of the future or from being fearful that we were not loved or accepted for who we were. They may also stem from any hurt or trauma we experienced in response to others' behaviour towards us, from feeling that we weren't heard or from knowing that we lacked power in a situation and felt helpless or from a general feeling that we were misunderstood. In adulthood, we display various behaviours, although they manifest in different ways, as a means of avoiding the pain we have brought with us from the past or might experience in the future. Whether we overeat to avoid our feelings or take drugs or drink excessively, or smoke. Whether we shop unnecessarily to make ourselves feel better or gamble or have sex outside a loving relationship. There are numerous ways we are either trying to avoid our feelings or trying to recapture a fleeting feeling of happiness, comfort and peace. We are basically looking for any opportunity to avoid the fear and pain of being a human being living in the world.

At some point in our lives, these avoidance mechanisms served a purpose, they insulated us from our real feelings and temporarily deluded us that all would be well. It may be, that at this point of our lives, we can start to recognise that these mechanisms that we thought were protecting us have become maladaptive and don't keep us safe at all but, potentially, cause us even greater pain than the actual pain we were hoping to avoid.

Not all of us go to extremes to avoid the pain of life but many of us recognise the behaviours we have adopted as an attempt to keep us away from the risk of pain. We might try to distract ourselves or ignore and deny that there is anything painful even going on. Finding compassion for ourselves when we are suffering by recognising that something hurts and being kind to ourselves in response (just like we would if we stubbed our toe – we would probably yelp from the pain and rub our toe until it felt better) doesn't take the pain away but embraces it and tries to accept the hurt. To try to resist the discomfort we feel, actually only makes the pain worse and increases our suffering. It is only through showing ourselves kind regard we can feel the pain and then be in a better position to let it go or allow it to dissipate naturally. This is the wellspring of self-compassion.

Recognising Our Feelings

Many of us aren't sure what we are actually feeling at any given time. There are lists of human emotions defined by psychologists and separated into main feelings and sub-categories. The six basic emotions are understood to be happiness, sadness, anger, fear, disgust and surprise. All other feelings are thought to be derived from these including affection, depression, frustration, hope, empathy, shame, love and gratitude.

It is easy to be confused as to which particular emotions we are experiencing because sometimes this is not reflected in our actual behaviour. We can find ourselves showing anger but at times this can be because we are really feeling scared or sad but find it harder to express these emotions. We can find ourselves displaying sadness when the circumstances may suggest that we should feel happy. Also, our feelings can be based on a mixture of emotions and are not always easy to categorise in a straightforward tick box exercise. At times, we aren't even aware of our underlying feelings and sometimes we don't feel any emotion at all, we are just in neutral. Sometimes hurt or grief can lie beneath the surface and, out of seemingly nowhere, up wells a wave of emotion that can take us by surprise. The important thing here is to try to become more alert to and aware of the emotions we are having, and just notice these with no judgement. To raise our awareness with interest and no criticism for how it is we might feel allows us to know ourselves more fully and accept both ourselves and our emotions, however difficult they might be.

In moments of suffering, whatever may cause them, we can try to allow our feelings to be present when it feels safe to do so, rather than turning our attention away. In recognising that we feel the way we do, with compassion for ourselves, we are being mindful. This stops us from overreacting and becoming consumed by our feelings. Our fears and anxieties can lessen when we recognise that we are human beings doing the best we can in any given moment. From this perspective, we can respond more effectively and objectively to the situation we find ourselves in.

It is important to acknowledge that whatever is going on in the present moment only exists in the here and now. Any thoughts we have about the past or the future are just that – thoughts. Any feelings we have are located in the present moment, regardless of the trigger. If we can recognise that the thoughts, feelings and behaviours we have are just physical and emotional sensations that can change and alter, whilst we stay calm and centred in our awareness, we are practising mindfulness.

To try to resist painful or difficult feelings often only heightens them. It is this resistance, which consumes a lot of our energy, which in turn often creates even stronger feelings of pain for us. We need to remind ourselves that we are not defined by how we feel and that feelings do and will pass. This includes the good feelings too! Nothing good lasts forever and neither does the bad, not in exactly the same form anyway. It bends and flows like a river, at moments seemingly unpassable, at other times it becomes more free flowing, easier to navigate and move through. One thing is for certain though, and that is to resist our emotions (and by this we mean, to deny them, push them away, divert our attention away from them or try to avoid them in countless different, usually unhealthy ways) we are actually causing ourselves more suffering and pain. We cannot really escape our feelings so our best option is to just experience our emotions, as they are, in the present moment.

Many of us have heard of compassion fatigue when we feel we just have no more resources available to give to others. Becoming mindful helps us to focus on what we are feeling or thinking right now, and by paying attention to this we can more clearly see or find what we ourselves might need in the moment. When we become able to meet our own needs more fully, we are more likely to feel we then have the resources to reach out to others. We are no longer depleted, our emotional and physical stocks are replenished and we can offer the same compassion to others as we are able to provide for ourselves. Equally, to allow ourselves to acknowledge how we feel, without judgement, in turn allows us to offer greater understanding and support to those around us.

All of us, as human beings, are designed to think and feel, these are processes that both keep us safe from harm and extend our ability to live successfully in this world. We do not have be a slave to our thoughts and emotions, but we can learn to respond to them with loving kindness. We can learn to recognise our common humanity and reframe a situation so we don't feel isolated by it. If we allow ourselves to feel the way we do, and we try not to resist our more challenging feelings, they will pass more swiftly. As it has been stated by many knowledgeable thinkers, "Pain is unavoidable but suffering is optional." As we increase our awareness of our emotions and form the habit of responding to any hurt we feel with compassion, the impact can be life changing.

Glimpsing Happiness

At times it can be difficult to comprehend that our natural state as human beings is not based on being ecstatically happy all the time. This is an unrealistic expectation but one that permeates Western culture and is perceived as a goal that can be achieved. If only we were wealthier, thinner, well regarded by others at all times, respected and admired, all would be well. If we set ourselves up to achieve all these things and more, the likelihood is that we will never be happy. To truly feel happy, often we need to appreciate all the good things we do have in life right at this moment, and show gratitude for the critical basics such as our good health and the well-being of our families. If we are lucky enough to have these things, then we are truly blessed.

Keeping what is really important, in the great scheme of things, in our minds can help us reduce the unrealistic and often unachievable set of goals and expectations we set ourselves. We no longer see ourselves as failures who are not meeting our own demands, and possibly those of others, but we are living, breathing human beings doing the best we can with what we have got. Having moments and glimpses of happiness in this life is a more achievable and realistic prospect. The cultivation of mindfulness can help us to recognise these moments more fully when they do come along, and this leads us to a deeper sense of satisfaction and appreciation for all we are lucky enough to have in our lives.

Cultivating the Mindfulness Habit

There is a well-known statement in the field of personal development that encourages us to ask that we may find the serenity to accept the things we cannot change, the courage to change the things we can and have the wisdom to know the difference. The wisdom to know the difference between what we can accept and what we need to change can come in the moments of reflection and clarity that developing a mindful practice can bring. We can incorporate these moments into some of our daily habits and rituals – waiting for the kettle to boil, brushing our teeth, walking the dog for example. We don't need to be sat cross-legged engaged in formal meditation practice to find a couple of minutes to be mindful. There are some suggestions for mindfulness practices you can try in the Further Resources section.

Sometimes just focusing on our breathing for thirty seconds can give us all the space we need to regroup and find some calm and peace in a hectic day.

Following the reflections in this journal can enable you to take a short amount of time out of your usual routine and focus your mind on the various aspects of cultivating self-compassion. This can become a healthy habit for us and give us the opportunity to take stock and be mindful so that we can train our minds to be as compassionate as they were intended to be. By completing this journal you are giving yourself the chance to create a sense of mindfulness in your life, just by spending five minutes reading the reflections that are offered. By completing the weekly journal pages, you are encouraged to stay with the process of becoming more self-compassionate in a way that works for you and fits around your life and commitments.

Each moment is a new beginning and we can make the changes in small but meaningful steps when we focus on creating a life with more compassion for ourselves, those around us and the wider world.

WEEKLY REFLECTIONS

AND JOURNAL PAGES

"The joy that compassion brings is one of the best kept secrets of humanity. It is a secret known only to very few people, a secret that has to be rediscovered over and over again."
Henri J.M. Nouwen

You have opened this reflective journal for a reason. You may hope to discover more about self-compassion and how this could assist you in your life. Maybe you have already gained some understanding in the practice of self-compassion and want to extend your learning further. Maybe you are hoping that self-compassion will bring you the peace and happiness you desire for yourself. You may recognise that to be able to give others authentic and sustainable compassion, we have to start by learning how to give compassion to ourselves.

There are no concepts covered that are difficult to comprehend. This journal will not try to complicate the issues or wrap up its key messages in hard to understand terms. It will not make the practice of self-compassion difficult for you or impossible to incorporate into your normal daily routine. This journal has been written for the knowledgeable and the novice alike.

There are no 'big reveals' in this journal! However, we do unlock the secret of compassion. The process of understanding how we can think, feel and behave with more compassion towards ourselves and others is relatively simple in its practice. By completing this journal and embarking on the path towards compassion, we and the world around us can fundamentally shift to a place of greater happiness and peace.

This week, how might I start to unlock the secret of compassion for myself?

What I think about this reflection:

How I feel about this reflection:

What I will do differently after considering this reflection:

What I am grateful for:

"Compassion is a verb."
Thich Nhat Hanh

We develop compassion for ourselves by simply making the commitment to develop compassion. We recognise that by being compassionate to ourselves, especially when it seems like the last thing on earth that we feel able to do, we can better get through the challenges that life throws at us.

By focusing on our shortcomings, failures and flaws we judge ourselves and treat ourselves harshly. Most of us would not treat anyone else in this way if they made a mistake or had difficulties. We would encourage and support them.

We need to apply this same logic to ourselves. Be kind and patient with ourselves. Consider and notice how we talk to ourselves – is our inner dialogue mostly critical or is it considerate and kind? Do we call ourselves names or berate ourselves on a regular basis both privately and publicly? How can we do this less and start to alter our internal and external dialogues, to encompass greater care and compassion for ourselves?

How can we start to recognise that we are doing our best, at times, in difficult circumstances? By trying to be our own best friend and treating ourselves with compassion, we won't change what is going on around us or anything that may have happened in the past, but we can change the way we see things and, in turn, how we respond to them now.

This week, how can I show myself compassion?

What I think about this reflection:

How I feel about this reflection:

What I will do differently after considering this reflection:

What I am grateful for:

"When we know ourselves to be connected to all others, acting compassionately is simply the natural thing to do."
Rachel Naomi Remen

At difficult moments, when we can recognise that we are not alone as human beings, we feel better. When we know that others have been through similar situations to those we might be going through, we feel it is possible to have hope that we will get through too. There is no situation or difficulty that exists that is not part of the shared human experience. This is why support groups offer better opportunities for people to recover or get through their challenges than by trying to get through them alone. This is especially the case when groups are run or attended by people who have been through a similar experience in life. Knowing we are not alone is a necessary part of our survival as a species.

In evolutionary terms we have to rely on each other. To survive childhood requires the care and attention of another human being. The times when we feel the happiest in our lives are usually when we have a strong sense of connection or bond to another or other people. We exist in family units for a reason. They help us, they give us a place to feel safe and belong.

All humans need very similar things. We are not so different as a race. When we feel connected to others we inevitably act in compassionate ways. When we love and care for others we can find a compassionate response. When we see another person suffering, we want to alleviate their pain. This is what connects us as humans, our innate ability to have and show compassion.

This week, how can I feel a stronger connection to all human beings?

What I think about this reflection:

How I feel about this reflection:

What I will do differently after considering this reflection:

What I am grateful for:

"Mindfulness and compassion actually develop at the same pace. The more mindful you become, the easier you'll find it to be compassionate."
Migyur Rinpoche

As we become more mindful by staying in the moment and focusing on doing the right thing right now, we find we are more able to know what we need at any given point in time. We can learn to respond to ourselves with greater levels of compassion than we thought possible. We can let go of things that we couldn't have previously. We can see more clearly why we behaved as we did in a particular situation, and not judge ourselves harshly for it.

Mindfulness and compassion go hand in hand. The more mindful we can be, the more compassionate we are able to become. The more focused we are on being compassionate towards ourselves and others, the more aware we are of our thoughts, feelings and behaviours. Mindfulness is not difficult, we just need to pay attention, that is all. We stop walking through life oblivious to what is going on within us and around us. We are noticing, without judgement. Even on the occasions when we do judge ourselves or others harshly, we notice with interest and compassion. We have opened our minds to the possibility of doing things differently for our own and the greater good.

This week, how can I pay attention to being mindful and compassionate towards myself and others?

What I think about this reflection:

How I feel about this reflection:

What I will do differently after considering this reflection:

What I am grateful for:

Consider your learning about self-compassion over the last four weeks.

Name three things you have learnt about compassion generally:

Name one key thing you have learnt about yourself:

How will what you have learnt benefit you?

What action would you like to take as a result of this learning?

Is there anything you would like to consider further?

"Simply accept ourselves with an open heart. To treat ourselves with the same kindness, caring and compassion we would show a good friend."
Kristin Neff

Many of us can show care and compassion to a friend in need when they are having a hard time. Our culture doesn't encourage us to show compassion to ourselves for fear that this could be classed as self-pitying behaviour. At times, especially at the beginning of a new phase in life, a short period of self-pity may be necessary for us to acknowledge that we are hurt or scared. As long as we then move through the self-pity to feel self-compassion for all we are going through, it is useful and beneficial. Only when we acknowledge the feelings that the situation is creating in us can we start the healing process. To resist, avoid or deny the feelings we have actually causes us greater pain and suffering.

How we look after ourselves, as we would a good friend, through the difficulties can make all the difference. Consider the ways you look after yourself when the going gets tough. What do you do to make yourself feel better? There are many ways we can provide ourselves with comfort. We can reassure ourselves that it is perfectly natural to feel the way we do rather than judge ourselves harshly. We can engage in activities that we find soothing and comforting such as walking in nature, listening to music or having a warm bath. Maybe talking to a trusted friend would help? We can take a self-compassion break for a couple of minutes to ask ourselves what we are feeling and what do we need in this moment? We can try to provide what we can for ourselves, including some reassurance or a few deep breaths.

This week, how can I treat myself as I would a good friend?

What I think about this reflection:

How I feel about this reflection:

What I will do differently after considering this reflection:

What I am grateful for:

"Compassion is not complete if it does not include oneself."
Allan Lokos

It is easy for most of us to understand why it is important to show others compassion, especially those we view as more vulnerable than ourselves. This ability is evolutionarily inherent to human beings; we are designed to be able to care for others. Unfortunately, the opposite is also true. We see mans' inhumanity to man playing out over and over again throughout history, and this still remains present in our current era.

How can we cultivate compassion towards ourselves so that we become complete and more able to be compassionate to others? Practising acts of self-kindness are not an excuse to be self-indulgent, but an opportunity to be respectful of our needs whilst fulfilling our obligations and responsibilities. We also need to learn how to forgive ourselves for not being perfect or for getting things wrong and making mistakes. These are what make us human beings rather than robots who have been programmed to perform in a particular way. Often we are driven by our biological need to belong, to fit in and to be valued by others.

One person who we will always belong with is actually ourself, and we can learn to value our own company and feelings. We can acknowledge that we don't always get everything right, but that we are doing our best and be willing to learn from our mistakes. Developing a kind, but responsible, approach to ourselves can create a shift in perspective that allows us to be the best we can be at any given time and in any given situation. Taking our own inventory, in a non-judgemental way, allows us to cultivate both self-acceptance and forgiveness for ourselves whilst acknowledging the impact of our behaviour on others. This is a truly responsible act of compassion.

This week, how can I take responsibility for my actions and show myself compassion?

What I think about this reflection:

How I feel about this reflection:

What I will do differently after considering this reflection:

What I am grateful for:

"Compassion is the keen awareness of the
interdependence of all things."
Thomas Merton

Compassion is defined as 'to suffer with'. Many of us can feel isolated
at times, and loneliness is known to be a significant risk factor when
it comes to our health and well-being. When we are able to develop
compassion for ourselves it means that we always have the ability to
find comfort and support from within, rather than be dependent on
external factors. However, we must also recognise how we are equal
and worthy contenders to all other human beings. We belong to the
human race, at all times, in all situations. Often it is easier to feel like
we belong in the good times rather than the more difficult ones.

We know that when we honestly share how we feel with others,
our burden lessens and even though the situation may not have
changed, we feel more capable of dealing with it. To reach out to
another human being may not only help us but it could help them too.
We need to keep building our networks, whether these relationships
are conducted face to face or digitally. We need to reach out and be
willing to let people support us when we are in need. We would try to
offer the same support with compassion wouldn't we? How could we
ask someone for support this week? Often, people are only too happy
to help.

This week, how can I recognise that we are all in this together and reach out to others and ask for help?

What I think about this reflection:

How I feel about this reflection:

What I will do differently after considering this reflection:

What I am grateful for:

"You can't stop the waves, but you can learn to surf."
Jon Kabat-Zinn

Life will happen to us – most of the time there is nothing we can do to stop it. At times we will fail in our endeavours and struggle with our losses. We will experience situations that were no fault of our own but that feel unfair and unkind, cruel even. How do we make peace with these inevitable aspects of what it means to be alive?

We can do nothing to change the past. Worrying about the future won't necessarily change it. To try and stay focused on this moment in time can help us negotiate what is to come to greater effect. The waves of challenge will keep coming at us. We can protect ourselves as best we can. We can think about how we approach the waves, how we respect the lessons they might teach us, we can try to draw out any positives that we can find. This is called survival.

By focusing on the here and now, at this very moment, we can choose to feel safe. We can choose to feel a sense of peace, and we can allow the wave to wash over us and not take us back out to sea with it.

This week, how can I keep my mind focused on all that is well in the present moment?

What I think about this reflection:

How I feel about this reflection:

What I will do differently after considering this reflection:

What I am grateful for:

Consider your learning about self-compassion over the last four weeks.

Name three things you have learnt about compassion generally:

Name one key thing you have learnt about yourself:

How will what you have learnt benefit you?

What action would you like to take as a result of this learning?

Is there anything you would like to consider further?

"If you want others to be happy, practice compassion. If you want to be happy, practice compassion."
Dalai Lama

Cultivating compassion for ourselves initially can be difficult. We need to not only plant the seeds for this change to take place in our lives, but also keep watering them and make sure they have everything they need to keep growing. We have to remind ourselves to focus on bringing more compassion into our lives. In all likelihood, we haven't necessarily been taught to do this, and in most cases we aren't encouraged to do this by the society we live in. In fact, often we are taught to do the opposite!

So compassion requires practice and lots of it! If we can just try to spend one minute each day practising compassion towards ourselves then it is likely to come more easily in time. When we can learn to give ourselves a break, rest when we need to, accomplish what we can in the timescales available and nourish ourselves in the ways that we require, we are actively treating ourselves with compassion and kindness.

When we can notice our behaviour, thoughts and feelings with no self-judgement, whilst acknowledging it when something hurts or doesn't feel ok, then we are treating ourselves with compassion.

This week, how can I practice acts of compassion towards myself to help me feel nurtured and cared for?

What I think about this reflection:

How I feel about this reflection:

What I will do differently after considering this reflection:

What I am grateful for:

"Talk to yourself like you would someone you love."
Brené Brown

Western culture often supports the myth that the harder we are on ourselves the more we will achieve. Actually, the opposite is true. Yes, we may need some degree of challenge because if everything was easy then we would never truly feel like we had achieved anything. We can give ourselves such a hard time for just being human, having feelings and emotions that we don't understand, or for not reaching the goals we have set ourselves. However, we mistakenly believe that by criticising ourselves we will achieve more; in actual fact this doesn't tend to motivate us to achieve anything, it just tends to make us feel bad about ourselves.

If we think of a friend, or even a child coming to us to say how badly they have done in a test of some sort, would we criticise them, shout at them, tell them how stupid they have been? Probably not, so why do we respond to our own inability to always succeed with harsh criticism and self-flagellation? We can learn to respond to ourselves in the loving and supportive way we would show to others when they are struggling.

The way we talk to ourselves can be the making or breaking of us. No one else hears the thoughts that go on in our heads so we can, all by ourselves, start to notice the critic when he or she appears and respond with gentle challenge. Punishing ourselves for getting things wrong isn't helpful, it is, in fact, damaging and means it is less likely we will achieve our goals and aspirations. To respond to ourselves with love, support and understanding, without removing the need to take responsibility for our actions, will take us a lot further and, in turn, help us to attain our aims.

This week, how can I talk to myself in a compassionate way, especially when I get something wrong or make a mistake?

What I think about this reflection:

How I feel about this reflection:

What I will do differently after considering this reflection:

What I am grateful for:

"Having compassion starts and ends with having compassion for all those unwanted parts of ourselves, all those imperfections that we don't even want to look at."
Pema Chodron

We all have to start somewhere on our journey towards having more compassion for ourselves. The underlying process is based on finding a sense of acceptance towards who we are and where we find ourselves in life. Many of the things that make us who we are we had no say in. Our genes, our upbringing, the society and culture in which we found ourselves were not chosen by us but create the foundation for who we become.

We do, however, need to take responsibility for looking at ourselves honestly, but crucially, without judgement. Not one of us is perfect in every way, and wouldn't life be boring if we were? We all have strengths and great things about us as well as aspects that we would rather were not there. But this is what makes us human. So rather than aspiring to perfection in every aspect of our lives, we can work towards accepting ourselves exactly as we are at this moment in time. Unique human beings, doing the best we can. Making a list of all the positive qualities we have may be helpful here as well as listing three aspects of ourselves we might like to change or develop.

This week, how can I recognise all my positive qualities and treat my imperfections with compassion and understanding?

What I think about this reflection:

How I feel about this reflection:

What I will do differently after considering this reflection:

What I am grateful for:

"Mindfulness is simply being aware of what is happening right now without wishing it were different."
James Baraz

As human beings we tend to seek out pleasure and avoid pain. This is an inevitable aspect of our psychophysiological make-up. When we feel happiness we want it to last forever, but this is an unrealistic expectation and impossible to maintain. When we feel uncomfortable or unpleasant emotions we try to avoid them. We do this in a myriad of ways. We can try and ignore how we feel and hope the feelings will go away. We can find ourselves engaging in more risky behaviours such as overeating, smoking, drug taking, drinking more alcohol than is good for us, engaging in greater amounts of sexual activity, gambling, addictively exercising and shopping for things we don't need. The list of avoidance behaviours we can engage in is endless! And we are prone to carry out any combination of behaviours that we know will either make us feel better or push the feelings we have away, albeit temporarily.

We learn to accept our feelings by practising mindfulness. This allows us to recognise the emotions, which can be a struggle in itself, especially after years of practising our well-honed avoidance mechanisms! By acknowledging the feeling we can start to try and accept it. Going through the good and bad, the highs and the lows, is part and parcel of life. But causing ourselves more suffering, by avoiding our feelings, can have devastating consequences.

The fact is that all feelings pass. Nothing stays fantastic forever. It's not called the 'honeymoon period' for nothing! Real life kicks in. We cannot avoid the trials and tribulations of life, otherwise known as reality. But the challenges pass too, and things don't always feel difficult. To accept what is happening and how we are feeling, without trying to change things, allows us the chance to move through life with fewer side effects.

This week, how can I accept what is happening right now without needing to change anything?

What I think about this reflection:

How I feel about this reflection:

What I will do differently after considering this reflection:

What I am grateful for:

Consider your learning about self-compassion over the last four weeks.

Name three things you have learnt about compassion generally:

Name one key thing you have learnt about yourself:

How will what you have learnt benefit you?

What action would you like to take as a result of this learning?

Is there anything you would like to consider further?

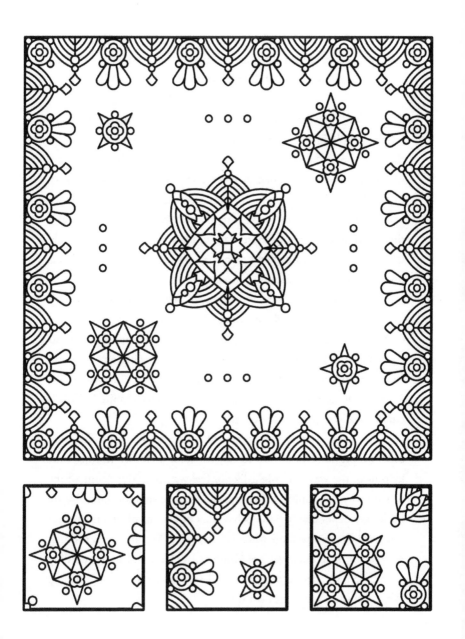

"Self-compassion is simply giving the same kindness to ourselves that we would give to others."
Christopher Germer

Many of us know that when required, we are able to show compassion for the people in our lives we are close to. We know that we try, to the best of our ability, to give compassion to our children, especially when they are young. When they suffer we are strongly moved to try to alleviate their suffering in any way we can. We provide guidance and warnings for them to be careful, to watch their step, to raise their awareness to the possibilities of injury or harm. We instinctively try to protect them from any pain that may come their way. This is unconditional compassion in action.

Within our immediate and extended families we may often try to support and show understanding when we see someone struggling or having a hard time. We may offer care and compassion to our friends at times of need. Often, when we are showing empathy and consideration for the other adults in our lives, a part of us would like to feel we would receive similar support should we require it. This is conditional compassion in action.

The reality is that sometimes when we are having difficulties, other people don't know how to help us or, for their own reasons, can't help us in the ways we might like or feel we need. This is one of the reasons why developing self-compassion can be so important. We are no longer dependent on the behaviours or actions of others to meet our need for compassion when we struggle. We can learn, through practice, to give ourselves the kindness, warmth and understanding we require. We can become more self-sufficient and self-supporting. We can always be on our own side.

This week, how can I show myself the kindness that I am able to give to others?

What I think about this reflection:

How I feel about this reflection:

What I will do differently after considering this reflection:

What I am grateful for:

"Compassion means full immersion in the condition
of being human."
Henri J.M. Nouwen

Being human is difficult. Once we accept this fact, it actually becomes a lot easier! We need to experience all aspects of the human condition, the joy, the pain, the highs and the lows as well as the mundane, to appreciate the good times and know we can get through the more challenging times.

To cultivate compassion, we need to recognise how hard it can be to be a human being. To have bodies and minds that may fail and will age. To lose those close to us. To struggle with change. To feel vulnerable and scared. Once we acknowledge that being human comes with its challenges, we can find empathy for ourselves and others during the difficult times. We can also choose to recognise these inherent parts of life and live as best we can, regardless.

This week, how can I acknowledge how challenging it is to be a human being?

What I think about this reflection:

How I feel about this reflection:

What I will do differently after considering this reflection:

What I am grateful for:

"Compassion is like a multivitamin for the mind."
Paul Gilbert

When we make a decision to focus on compassion this week, whether it is to cultivate it for ourselves or find it in ourselves to give to others, we have already achieved a great deal. By practising compassion in recognising our own needs and trying to meet these ourselves, it is like taking a daily dose of self-care and self-regard.

It's not always the big things that make the difference. Sometimes it's the tiny things that help us feel kinder towards ourselves and more respectful of our needs. Maybe we make a conscious decision to have an early night when we feel tired so we feel well rested the next day or we focus on having a healthy meal. Maybe we choose to go for a walk in the fresh air, exercise in a way we enjoy or have a hot bath with bubbles to encourage a feeling of relaxation. Maybe we read a good book or call a friend for a chat. The more we practice being in the moment, thinking about what we need right now and how to give ourselves compassion, the more readily and easily the focus on our needs becomes. If something difficult happens or is going on in our lives, when we can stop and acknowledge that what just happened hurt, with no judgement for ourselves for feeling the way we do, then we are getting closer to practising self-compassion.

When we recognise our own needs, we can learn to more easily recognise and meet the needs of others. It is also in the small ways which we can assist others that shows our compassion for them. Whether it is the offer of support at a difficult time, smiling at someone or holding their hand for a few minutes, we can try any number of tiny, yet compassionate gestures, and make the world of difference to another person in that moment.

This week, how can I perform small acts of compassion towards myself and those around me?

What I think about this reflection:

How I feel about this reflection:

What I will do differently after considering this reflection:

What I am grateful for:

"We have to make mistakes, it's how we learn
compassion for others."
Curtis Sittenfeld

We all make mistakes. Sometimes we say and do things without thinking about their impact or how we might make other people feel. We are human beings who don't always get things right.

When we make amends and sincerely apologise for our behaviour, this doesn't take the hurt we may have caused away. It does, however, at least recognise our wrongdoing. It helps us to be more considerate in the future, and for others to trust that our intentions are good and honourable.

When others make mistakes towards us we can find it hard to forgive them, even if an apology is presented to us. In our interactions with others, we all inevitably make mistakes. We can deepen our self-understanding through these errors and try to forgive ourselves and others. For the most part, we are all just doing our best.

This week, how can I try to forgive myself and others for any hurt we may cause?

What I think about this reflection:

How I feel about this reflection:

What I will do differently after considering this reflection:

What I am grateful for:

Consider your learning about self-compassion over the last four weeks.

Name three things you have learnt about compassion generally:

Name one key thing you have learnt about yourself:

How will what you have learnt benefit you?

What action would you like to take as a result of this learning?

Is there anything you would like to consider further?

"Whatever the present moment contains, accept it as if you had chosen it. Always work with it, not against it."
Eckhart Tolle

To practise mindfulness as a means of creating more compassion for ourselves, we need to bring our focus to the present moment. When our emotions are running high or our mood is low, this can feel like a challenge too far. Reminding ourselves to be mindful in the moment can sometimes be all we need to trigger the response to stop and observe how we are feeling.

All we have to do is pay attention to the moment. Quiet our minds and when possible, still our bodies, to focus on our breath entering and leaving. After only a minute or two of noticing this fundamental function our bodies naturally perform, we will feel our minds start to clear and the feelings start to lift. We are not working against the emotion, we are just feeling it and trying to accept it.

To neither suppress nor exaggerate our feelings is the key to practising mindful compassion. When we can feel our pain but not be controlled by it, or enjoy a moment of peace but not hold too tightly to it, we are working with our feelings and not against them.

This week, how can I accept how I feel in the present moment?

What I think about this reflection:

How I feel about this reflection:

What I will do differently after considering this reflection:

What I am grateful for:

"In deep self-acceptance grows a compassionate understanding."
Jack Kornfield

How wonderful a feeling it is to truly accept ourselves! At first, when we start on the journey towards self-acceptance, the road can seem too steep and too difficult to navigate. Expect some resistance and discomfort. Keep trying anyway. With gentle steps towards the goal of accepting ourselves and recognising all we uniquely bring to a situation, we start to find the road a little easier.

This journey towards self-acceptance is not a linear one. None of us move forwards in a series of easy steps that clearly occur one after the other. We might move forwards and then go back a few steps. In fact many of us find ourselves in what feels like a worse place than when we started at times! The important thing is to recognise that this is all movement, even if sometimes it appears to be in the wrong direction!

When we want to grow as human beings, learn more about ourselves and how we engage with the world, the lessons can be hard. But this is no reason to give up or feel disillusioned. The path towards deep self-acceptance is a lifetime's work, and it's all about progress not perfection.

This week, how can I be more accepting of myself and recognise all the progress I have made on my journey so far?

What I think about this reflection:

How I feel about this reflection:

What I will do differently after considering this reflection:

What I am grateful for:

"Compassion is not a religious business, it is a human business. It is not a luxury, it is essential for our own peace and mental stability. It is essential for human survival."
Dalai Lama

We don't need to be religious to have compassion. Although at the core of all the major world religions, compassion is a key teaching. In a secular life, we can still find compassion for ourselves and others as human beings.

Discovering self-compassion can be a life altering experience. We can find long term and deeply meaningful ways of practising compassion when we choose to recognise the necessity of this for peace of mind. We can learn to think, feel and act in new ways that show the compassion we are cultivating for ourselves and, in turn, others.

If we, as a human race, can learn to have greater compassion towards ourselves and those around us, then the impact of this could fundamentally shift the way the world operates. For humanity to survive, as well as thrive, cultivating compassion holds the key.

This week, how will I do my best to cultivate compassion for myself and all of my fellow human beings?

What I think about this reflection:

How I feel about this reflection:

What I will do differently after considering this reflection:

What I am grateful for:

"Self-acceptance is my refusal to be in an adversarial
relationship with myself."
Nathaniel Branden

At times, we might recognise that no one can be as tough on us as we are on ourselves. Very few of us, in our adulthood, have other people who explicitly state their great expectations of us directly towards us on a regular basis. We might get a sense of what others want from us and how they would like us to lead our lives. We might feel other's criticism and condemnation even for how we choose to behave or act in the world. But if we aren't hurting anyone else, as adults, no one has the right to tell us what to do.

How we internalise these criticisms can cause us great pain and suffering. So even if we haven't got these critics around us on a daily basis, we can continue to extend their harsh judgement and demands towards ourselves regardless. Maybe we feel like we will never live up to others' expectations of us. We might often feel like we won't live up to our own expectations of ourselves.

Until we can step off the wheel of self-criticism and punishing expectations, we cannot truly accept ourselves. To focus on all that we are not, instead of all that we are, leads us to a depressive and anxious state of mind. To make no comparisons of ourselves to others and to care less what others think of us is a helpful step towards greater self-acceptance. To stop berating ourselves for what we haven't yet achieved and to resist revering ideals that do not provide deep and long-lasting happiness, takes us further. To remember how far we have come and how much we have achieved, sometimes through difficult circumstances, takes us further still.

This week, how can I accept myself and my current situation in life without judgement?

What I think about this reflection:

How I feel about this reflection:

What I will do differently after considering this reflection:

What I am grateful for:

Consider your learning about self-compassion over the last four weeks.

Name three things you have learnt about compassion generally:

Name one key thing you have learnt about yourself:

How will what you have learnt benefit you?

What action would you like to take as a result of this learning?

Is there anything you would like to consider further?

"My mission in life is not merely to survive, but to thrive; and
to do so with some passion, some compassion,
some humour, and some style."
Maya Angelou

In the Western world, we are mostly lucky and privileged enough to have the resources we need to survive at a basic level. We have clean water to drink and, for the fortunate amongst us, a roof over our heads. We have mostly some opportunity for gainful employment or voluntary work. We have access to healthcare and reasonably priced food. Our children receive an education. We are governed democratically, we have legally binding human rights and are protected by both the law and the enforcement agencies. These are the basic tenets required for a human being to survive.

We need to appreciate all we have and how we can, at times, take many of these things for granted. Sometimes it can feel like all we are doing is surviving, getting through each day as best we can. We can still find ourselves asking how we can find the deeper meaning in life.

Finding what makes us feel passionate, whether it is a cause or an activity, can help. What makes us feel alive? How can we find compassion for ourselves and others? How can we laugh more and have more fun? How can we add a touch of our own unique style to every situation we are in? How can we move through our lives without feeling the need to make apologies for being who we are? Answering these questions, or even just considering them, can help move us beyond pure survival to a place where we can feel more fully alive.

This week, how can I increase my opportunities to thrive in life?

What I think about this reflection:

How I feel about this reflection:

What I will do differently after considering this reflection:

What I am grateful for:

"If you have no compassion for yourself then you are not able to develop compassion for others."
Dalai Lama

To authentically give compassion to others, for no other reason and with no direct benefit to ourselves, is impossible without compassion for ourselves. To be without an agenda during any human interaction takes true self-compassion. We can listen to others with the hope that they may listen to us. We can give to others in the hope that they will give to us. We have so many conditions on what we do but most of the time we are not even aware of these. We have maybe never even thought about it.

To give to others, completely unconditionally, can be difficult mainly as it feels so unfamiliar. To give, just for giving's sake, is not something we are taught to do in our competitive culture. We can manage it more easily when our children are young, but we also want things back from them in return as they grow, such as acceptable behaviour, good grades and tidy bedrooms. This is part of the way we train our young to behave in the world. Children need this information and to have these responsible behaviours reinforced, but they also need to feel accepted and loved exactly as they are. Just as we do.

This week, how can I give compassion unconditionally to myself and others?

What I think about this reflection:

How I feel about this reflection:

What I will do differently after considering this reflection:

What I am grateful for:

"If all you did was put your hand on your heart and wish yourself well, it would be a moment well spent."
Elisha Goldstein

How often do any of us stop for a moment and wish ourselves well? In our culture, society and communities this behaviour generally isn't taught or encouraged. It might be seen as self-indulgent or even unnecessary. However, who could argue that to feel safe and secure within ourselves as we go about our business is a bad thing? To wish ourselves well, not at anyone else's expense or at a cost to another, can only be an act of self-compassion that has a resoundingly positive effect on our health and well-being and, in turn, the lives of those around us.

A specific act of kindness towards ourselves, especially when things feel a bit out of control or we are struggling, can ground us and bring us back to a place of safety. We are not dependent on others to provide this, we can simply give ourselves the warmth and understanding we need as a human being to keep going through life with a sense of security. To have this self-protection and care mechanism, acting as a support system in our lives on a daily basis, we find that we are more fully able to wish others well and happy.

This week, what can I do to wish myself well?

What I think about this reflection:

How I feel about this reflection:

What I will do differently after considering this reflection:

What I am grateful for:

"If we can be mindful of our fears and anxieties rather than over-identifying with them, we can save ourselves a lot of unwarranted pain."
Kristin Neff

How we relate to our feelings can make a significant difference to how we deal with them. When we get caught up in the emotions of fear and anxiety, they can exert a huge amount of control over us. If we can learn to see our feelings as just that – feelings – they have a lot less power and we can manage them more successfully.

Often we aren't even sure what emotion we are feeling or why we are feeling the way we do. Our fears and anxieties can often come out sideways as we struggle to understand them. For example, when we feel angry, it can be due to an underlying feeling of sadness or hurt. How often are we able to see this clearly? For most of us, not that often! We just let the feeling of anger overtake us and, at times, act on it.

Taking a moment to acknowledge how we feel, without judgement, can be liberating. When we judge or criticise ourselves for whatever reason, we do ourselves more harm than good. If we can start to realise that whatever we feel is just a feeling and that it will pass, then we can save ourselves a lot of additional pain and distress. To be able to say to ourselves or someone else that we feel scared or anxious about something acknowledges the feeling without allowing it to define us as a human being. To stay in the moment and try to accept our emotions, with warmth and understanding, allows us the opportunity to gain clarity. Once we have this insight we are more likely to remain in control, hold ourselves in check and not act on our feelings indiscriminately, either towards ourselves or others.

This week, how can I accept my painful feelings and hold them in non-judgemental awareness?

What I think about this reflection:

How I feel about this reflection:

What I will do differently after considering this reflection:

What I am grateful for:

Consider your learning about self-compassion over the last four weeks.

Name three things you have learnt about compassion generally:

Name one key thing you have learnt about yourself:

How will what you have learnt benefit you?

What action would you like to take as a result of this learning?

Is there anything you would like to consider further?

"Our hearts have a limitless capacity for caring and compassion."
Anne Wilson-Schaef

If we ever consider ourselves to be fatigued by the amount of challenges we face, be assured that we are only sent what we can deal with. Our ability to overcome difficulty is the essential part of our nature of which we need to remind ourselves when the going gets tough. It is only through the challenge that we grow – in fact it's the hard knocks that send us further than the pats on the back at times. All human beings face difficulty. We are never alone in these challenging times; our common humanity binds us together. There are many people going through much worse than we are too, all over the world, right at this moment. That doesn't mean our pain and difficulty is invalid, it can just put certain elements into perspective.

The human experience is never perfect for anyone, whether they are celebrities in their field or wealthy beyond measure. Everyone is fighting their own battle. We need to come to terms with the fact that suffering is an inevitable part of life, for us all. By accepting this and recognising that life is difficult, it can actually become much easier.

Who do we know who is having a hard time at the moment? How might we reach out to them and let them know they are cared for? This might not change their situation, but it can make all the difference to how they respond if they know they are not alone. When we extend our capacity to give to others, even if we are struggling ourselves, we will have achieved something wonderful.

This week, how can I show my care and compassion to all those I come into contact with?

What I think about this reflection:

How I feel about this reflection:

What I will do differently after considering this reflection:

What I am grateful for:

"As you breathe in, cherish yourself. As you breathe out, cherish all beings."
Dalai Lama

The breath is such a powerful force. It is the difference between life and death. With no breath, there is no life. We can harness this power to help us focus on compassion. Very simply, by focusing on compassion for ourselves when we inhale and compassion for others when we exhale.

As we continuously breathe, whatever we are doing and wherever we are going, we can practise this mindful behaviour anyplace, anytime, anywhere. We can be in a meeting, in the car, walking the dog, showering, making dinner, going to sleep. Bringing our attention to our breath and focusing on cherishing ourselves can help us feel at peace and give us a renewed sense of vim and vigour in the world. This simple practice cultivates compassion for both ourselves and others.

This week, how can I bring my attention to my breathing and value myself and others in the process?

What I think about this reflection:

How I feel about this reflection:

What I will do differently after considering this reflection:

What I am grateful for:

"A vision of what I could have, what I could do, who I could be
has emerged if I allow my heart to become a place of compassion,
acceptance and forgiveness."
Sharon E Rainey

All of us, at times, have said or done something we have regretted or felt ashamed of. By acknowledging this and accepting it – we can't change the past after all – and having compassion for ourselves rather than criticising and condemning ourselves, we can actively change how we might approach a similar situation if it were to occur again.

Often we mull over things we have said or done and judge ourselves too harshly because we are scared that others are judging us. For the most part they are usually too busy judging themselves! By letting go of our own harsh self-judgements and treating ourselves with compassion, we are free to be ourselves again. We will not always get things right. As long as we recognise when we need to make amends by apologising and trying to do the best we can in all situations, we can learn to forgive ourselves and move on. Are there any amends you would like to make this week? There are many ways we can do this but the process of self-forgiveness starts with the acknowledgement that amends are required. Often, the person we need to forgive the most is ourself.

This week, how can I forgive myself and make amends for any hurt I have caused?

What I think about this reflection:

How I feel about this reflection:

What I will do differently after considering this reflection:

What I am grateful for:

"You yourself, as much as anybody in the entire universe, deserve your love and affection."
Gautama Buddha

For the most part we can recognise that other people are worthy of love, especially the people we choose as friends and partners and the children we have in our lives. When we can clearly see that we ourselves are also completely entitled to feel loved and cared for, we are practising self-compassion.

Some of us find ourselves in a variety of relationships with people who we aren't sure about. We aren't certain that they show us the care and consideration we feel we deserve. When we practise self-compassion it empowers us to move away from those who don't give us the respect and recognition we require. We can more easily recognise who we want in our lives and who we need to distance ourselves from. It is not for us to sit in judgement of those around us, but to make our boundaries for others' behaviours clear – what we are willing and unwilling to accept. This behaviour, when it is well intentioned, commands the respect of others but, most of all, shows that we have self-respect.

We all deserve to feel love and affection rather than criticism and disregard. This process starts with how we treat and value ourselves.

This week, how can I show myself love and affection by valuing myself more?

What I think about this reflection:

How I feel about this reflection:

What I will do differently after considering this reflection:

What I am grateful for:

Consider your learning about self-compassion over the last four weeks.

Name three things you have learnt about compassion generally:

Name one key thing you have learnt about yourself:

How will what you have learnt benefit you?

What action would you like to take as a result of this learning?

Is there anything you would like to consider further?

"We do not need any sort of religious orientation to lead a life that is ethical, compassionate and kind."
Sharon Salzberg

Bringing our focus to behaving in an ethical, compassionate and kind manner during our daily existence is not based on religious doctrine, but human doctrine. To limit the amount of pain and suffering we might cause to others is an important ethical practice. If we can focus on the small ways we can make a difference to the other beings that share our world, as well as respecting the earth itself, then we are contributing to the possibility that there will be resources available for generations to come.

By doing the simple things like recycling where possible and buying ethical and organic products we are making a privileged and informed choice. Not everyone is in the position to make such choices, but where we can we would all like to. We all want the world to be a better, kinder, safer and more sustainable and compassionate place for all our children. Our small acts of kindness and compassion can make a big difference.

This week, in what small ways can I be ethical, compassionate and kind?

What I think about this reflection:

How I feel about this reflection:

What I will do differently after considering this reflection:

What I am grateful for:

"Angry is just Sad's bodyguard."
Liza Palmer

Experiencing emotion is part and parcel of what it means to be a human being. We generally aren't taught to recognise this fact as we go through life responding to the situations, people and circumstances we find ourselves in and around.

We can struggle to identify what the emotion we are having actually is. It is hard to pinpoint our feelings. They are often a confusing mix of different emotions all rolled up in one hard to understand clump. What often presents as the most obvious emotion, such as anger, is in actual fact our response to feeling hurt or sad. We think we feel anger but we are just expressing what comes most naturally to us rather than what we are actually feeling. Many times the hurt, pain or sadness we experience is so uncomfortable for us that we, almost as an automatic response mechanism, express a more socially acceptable emotion instead. We struggle to know what to do with the feelings that we are least used to dealing with, and it is therefore perfectly understandable that we then find it difficult to identify them, let alone express them in their pure form.

The practice of mindfulness allows us to stay quiet for long enough to reflect on the emotions that are present for us in any given moment. We gain clarity by focusing on our breath in a way that can empower us and allow us to just experience the emotions, whatever they may be. We can allow waves of happiness, sadness, hope, fear and gratitude wash over us. We are not held in their grip, acting out on any of our emotions without insight. The more we practise understanding the emotions we feel the more able we are to let them go.

This week, how can I know and accept my feelings, whatever they may be?

What I think about this reflection:

How I feel about this reflection:

What I will do differently after considering this reflection:

What I am grateful for:

"Compassion is not a virtue – it is a commitment. It is not something we have or don't have, it's something we choose to practice."
Brené Brown

People might view being compassionate as a virtue. It is actually a decision. We can decide to focus on the ways we can be more compassionate to both ourselves and others. We can wake up in the morning and repeat a short phrase to remind ourselves of our commitment to being the best person we can be on that day, and to include ourselves and others in our circle of compassion.

Each day we can make a choice of how to live our lives. Every day we can choose again, a clean slate, a new way of being. Yes, we may have got things wrong in the past. We can't change this, but we can make a better choice today.

This week, how can I actively choose to live my life based on compassionate principles?

What I think about this reflection:

How I feel about this reflection:

What I will do differently after considering this reflection:

What I am grateful for:

"Understanding of and having compassion for ourselves and others
is the key to play, to joy, to bliss."
Amy Jalapeno

Discovering our capacity for compassion for both ourselves and others can allow us to be more present in every situation we find ourselves in. It allows us to be our real selves, without the need to try to impress others or aspire to be something we are not. It takes away the pressure to conform to other people's standards. It stops us focusing on other people's views of us. We no longer need to seek their approval or try to present an image with their views in mind.

In this regard, experiencing self-compassion is liberating. It frees us to be ourselves and to know that we are good enough. Not perfect maybe, but enough exactly as we are. We don't need to focus on other's views of us anymore; our own view of ourselves has taken precedence. We can play more freely, not worried if others see us make mistakes or make fools of ourselves. We can laugh and enjoy life more when we aren't focusing on what other people think of us. It is a state of bliss not to feel the need to act for the approval of others.

This week, how can I find more joy by caring less what others may think of me?

What I think about this reflection:

How I feel about this reflection:

What I will do differently after considering this reflection:

What I am grateful for:

Consider your learning about self-compassion over the last four weeks.

Name three things you have learnt about compassion generally:

Name one key thing you have learnt about yourself:

How will what you have learnt benefit you?

What action would you like to take as a result of this learning?

Is there anything you would like to consider further?

"Mindfulness brings us fully alive to the now of our conscious existence, the only place we actually exist!"
Paul Gilbert

To be mindful just means to focus on the present moment. The only moment that is real is the one we find ourselves in right now. As we try to become more fully conscious human beings, we need to harness the power of now. Nothing before this moment counts and anything that comes after this moment is unknown. All we can be certain of is right here and right now.

At various points during our waking hours we can choose to focus on the present moment. This is a powerful tool for cultivating mindfulness. We can take the time to meditate and just focus on the breath entering and leaving our bodies. We can follow a guided meditation that takes us through a series of steps. We can also follow mindful practices that we incorporate into our daily habits and routines.

Any experience we bring to practising mindfulness is useful. The more we can focus on the present moment, the less we worry and fret about the past or the future. The calmer our minds become, the more able we are to deal with the next thing that life demands of us.

The practice of mindfulness acts as the light and nourishment required for the seeds of compassion for ourselves and others to grow. In all likelihood, the more successfully we incorporate any formal or informal mindfulness practice into our lives, the richer and more meaningful our experiences become.

This week, how can I keep bringing my attention to the present moment?

What I think about this reflection:

How I feel about this reflection:

What I will do differently after considering this reflection:

What I am grateful for:

"Compassion is the key to the ultimate survival of our species."
Doug Dillon

Sometimes, to make ourselves feel better we put other people down. We are taught, in our culture, that to thrive we must always win and we can feel threatened when we think others are doing better than we are. We can find ourselves competing in many aspects of our lives from parenting to career development to the house we live in, the holidays we take, the clothes we wear and the car we drive. We no longer have to try to display our wealth on the outside when we feel so much richer on the inside. We don't have to engage in keeping up appearances when we know that our true value resides in the compassion we can show ourselves and others. This includes not feeling any satisfaction from other people's misfortune, but instead finding real empathy and compassion for their challenges.

At times we can distance ourselves from people who we feel are doing better than us because to acknowledge them may make us feel bad about ourselves. How can we acknowledge that others' success does not diminish our own? The groups we belong to can also allow us to separate ourselves from others, whether this is based on religious views or professional expertise. How might we recognise our similarities rather than our differences to others? Mostly the way that we make comparisons and set ourselves apart from any other person or group can cause us pain. Often, as human beings, the ties that bind us together are stronger than those that would tear us apart.

This week, how can I have compassion for all my fellow human beings wherever they are on their journey?

What I think about this reflection:

How I feel about this reflection:

What I will do differently after considering this reflection:

What I am grateful for:

"If your compassion does not include yourself, it is incomplete."
Jack Kornfield

For many of us being compassionate towards others is much easier than being compassionate towards ourselves. We are evolutionarily designed to give care and compassion to our young. This is how we have survived and thrived as a human species. We are not well versed, however, in including ourselves in this compassionate behaviour.

We need to make an active decision to become more compassionate towards ourselves. We have heard the ways we talk to ourselves at times, and we would probably never speak in such a harsh and unforgiving way to anyone else. We think that to treat ourselves so severely will motivate and push us further. Sometimes this may be the case, but not often. In fact, it is more likely to damage our resolve to reach a goal than propel us towards it.

When we speak to ourselves more kindly and recognise that, for the most part, we are doing the very best we can, then we are more likely to give ourselves the support and compassion we need to get things done and reach our goals.

This week, how can I make a conscious effort to be compassionate towards myself?

What I think about this reflection:

How I feel about this reflection:

What I will do differently after considering this reflection:

What I am grateful for:

"Forget the perfect offering. Everything is flawed. It's the cracks that let the light in."
Leonard Cohen

None of us are perfect, that is not what it means to be human. Equally, no one we come into contact with is perfect either. We are all flawed human beings, for the most part, doing the best we can. When we try to create a 'perfect' illusion of who we are, we are heading for disaster. It is truly exhausting to need to be seen as perfect in other people's eyes as well as our own. If we can accept we are doing our best and that our best is 'good enough', we are practising self-compassion.

The flaws we have are what make us real people rather than artificially created robots. The physical scars we have remind us of what we have survived. It is a similar scenario for our emotional scars, only these aren't as easy to see with the naked eye. We know what we have been through. We don't need to compare our journey to that of others. We are each entitled to wear our scars with pride. They show how far we have come and all that we have overcome. We are still standing regardless of the trauma we have had to endure.

Only when we can be honest with ourselves about our flawed bodies and minds, coupled with acceptance and gratitude, can we experience a true sense of peace.

This week, how can I appreciate and value my imperfections?

What I think about this reflection:

How I feel about this reflection:

What I will do differently after considering this reflection:

What I am grateful for:

Consider your learning about self-compassion over the last four weeks.

Name three things you have learnt about compassion generally:

Name one key thing you have learnt about yourself:

How will what you have learnt benefit you?

What action would you like to take as a result of this learning?

Is there anything you would like to consider further?

"Acknowledging the good that you already have in your life is the foundation of all abundance."
Eckhart Tolle

At times, we take the most important aspects of life for granted. We aspire to greater material wealth and compete endlessly to achieve status and recognition in our chosen fields. We can go through life ignoring the fact that if we have good health, we have already won the lottery. And that's what life can be, a lottery. Even when we treat our minds and bodies as well as we can, unfortunately, they can still fail and will inevitably age and suffer in any number of different ways. When we realise that we are all equally vulnerable to the fragility of being human, our focus can radically alter and we can find ourselves grateful for the smallest, but critically most important, basic elements of life.

We acknowledge the good we have in our lives by developing a sense of gratitude. This can be as simple as feeling grateful to have woken up in the morning, to recognising how we have overcome some of the challenges we have faced. The most important aspects of our busy lives are the most consistent such as family, health and home. We can feel truly blessed for the good health and well-being of those we love and care for. If we are lucky enough to have a place we can call home, we can feel immensely grateful. If we live in a country where we feel safe and protected, we are fortunate indeed. We can take these aspects of our lives for granted, but many others would see them as an impossible dream.

When we can truly feel humble for all that we have, we create and attract even greater possibilities for ourselves. We keep what we have by giving it away, whether this is our time and effort or our kindness and consideration. The more we express our gratitude the better we all feel.

This week, how can I recognise all that is good in my life and express my gratitude for this?

What I think about this reflection:

How I feel about this reflection:

What I will do differently after considering this reflection:

What I am grateful for:

"Wherever I go I talk to people about the need to be aware of the oneness of humanity."
Dalai Lama

When we consider ourselves to be distinct individuals we can more readily see our differences. We have different personalities, genes, looks, styles and preferences. We have different circumstances, incomes, homes, jobs, aspirations, religions, interests and habits. It is, in fact, sometimes easier to see our differences as individuals than it is to see our similarities.

However, we are all equal members of the same species, the same human race. This is the tie that binds us together as one. Many of us struggle, no one gets through their life without challenge of some description. Most of us want the world to be a better, safer and fairer place. All of us want our children to thrive and lead healthy and long, happy lives. To spend more time focusing on our similarities, our shared experiences and hopes for the future can help us recognise that we are one human race. When we have a sense of unity that comes from recognising we are all fully-fledged members of humanity, we can feel a deep bond with others in the world and, in turn, consider how we can help our fellow human beings.

To feel connected to our fellow inhabitants who share this planet can bring us a sense of belonging and common purpose that inspires us to keep going even when the challenge feels overwhelming. There is no experience we could have or any situation we could face that someone, somewhere hasn't found themselves in before us. The fact that we are not alone can shelter us in a storm.

This week, how can I focus on my connection to the whole of the human race?

What I think about this reflection:

How I feel about this reflection:

What I will do differently after considering this reflection:

What I am grateful for:

"With mindfulness, you can establish yourself in the
present in order to touch the wonders of life that are available
in that moment."
Nhat Hanh

Often we just stumble through life without acknowledging any of
the wonders that exist. The practice of mindfulness, being present in
the moment, can allow us the opportunity to realise what lies within
us and around us. Our bodies, perfectly adapted by thousands of
generations of evolutionary development function and allow us the
opportunity to thrive in our environment. The earth itself, provides us
with all we need to flourish and reproduce. These are the big wonders!

The smaller wonders of life can often get missed too. The beauty
of a sunrise and the shapes the clouds form in the sky. To hear the
sound of laughter and see the smile on someone's face. A cat purring
in contentment or a dog wagging its tail with uncomplicated joy.
To feel no physical discomfort or pain. To know there is food in the
fridge. To have a front door that can be closed and a roof that doesn't
let in the elements. To have a friend we can call upon to say hello.
To be able to see, hear, speak, smell, touch – all breathtaking in their
simplicity.

Often we only realise the wonders of life when their existence
is threatened. Sometimes we only appreciate what we have when we
face losing it. We can take the wonders of life, as well as life itself, for
granted. Mindfulness allows us the opportunity to experience and
appreciate all that we are and all that we have around us in the present
moment. What a gift!

This week, how can I stay in the present moment to fully appreciate all the wonders of life?

What I think about this reflection:

How I feel about this reflection:

What I will do differently after considering this reflection:

What I am grateful for:

"Compassion is the ultimate and most meaningful embodiment of emotional maturity. It is through compassion that a person achieves the highest peak and the deepest reach in his or her search for self-fulfilment."

Arthur Jersild

We would all like to think that, as adults, we are emotionally mature. However, sometimes our thoughts and actions defy this myth and we get a glimpse of how we can still operate from a place of childish confusion and recklessness. Directing compassion towards ourselves and others allows us the opportunity to foresee the consequences of our behaviour before we act. When we see children behave with compassion towards themselves or others we can feel full of admiration for their insight and maturity. It is no different for us in adulthood.

Recognising that we are all on a journey called life, which has ups and downs at every stage, but knowing that we are focused on bringing greater levels of compassion into our lives through our thoughts, feelings and actions, enables us to find a deeper level of self-fulfilment than we ever knew possible. To accept ourselves and the place we are at on our journey, with compassion and understanding for how we got here and all we have achieved, allows us to see more clearly how much further we can go. It also allows us to be more accepting and compassionate towards others, at whatever stage they are at on their journey.

This week, how can I find a deeper sense of compassion for myself and others to help me on my journey towards self-fulfilment?

What I think about this reflection:

How I feel about this reflection:

What I will do differently after considering this reflection:

What I am grateful for:

Consider your learning about self-compassion over the last four weeks.

Name three things you have learnt about compassion generally:

Name one key thing you have learnt about yourself:

How will what you have learnt benefit you?

What action would you like to take as a result of this learning?

Is there anything you would like to consider further?

"Imperfections are not inadequacies; they are reminders that
we are all in this together."
Brené Brown

We are all flawed. Not one of us can be, or ever will be, perfect in the ways we think, feel and act. Nor will we ever look or present ourselves perfectly, we all have imperfections. Equally, our lives will be never be without a flaw of some sort. There will always be an aspect that we would change if we could. This is the same for every one of us, the world over.

When we think our imperfections equate to inadequacy, somehow indicating that we are lacking or our value is less than that of others, we step into the realm of feeling isolated and alone. When we weigh ourselves up in comparison to others, either as the people we are or the external elements that we think define us, we are playing a game where there are no winners. It's like comparing apples and oranges – yes, both fruit grown from trees, and both valuable, but in completely different ways.

Self-compassion allows us to recognise our imperfections without judging ourselves for them. We can see our flaws and recognise the areas we might like to improve in our lives, but we know that these do not define us as human beings. This approach allows us to also accept the flaws in others and refrain from judging or blaming them for having these imperfections. We are reminded that none of us are perfect and on this basis we are all in this together.

This week, how can I recognise imperfections, without judgement, as evidence that we are all connected?

What I think about this reflection:

How I feel about this reflection:

What I will do differently after considering this reflection:

What I am grateful for:

"The path of compassion leads to the development of insight. But it doesn't work to say, "Ready, set, go! Be compassionate!" Beginning any practice depends on intention."

Sylvia Boorstein

We all have the occasional light bulb moments, when we are suddenly presented with a piece of information about ourselves that explains why we think, feel and behave the way we do at times. Real insight can grow when we make it our mission to practise self-compassion.

The growth towards becoming more compassionate is not always easy and does not regularly provide life shattering comprehension and recognition. It is a road of many twists and turns; sometimes we feel we are making great strides, other times we feel like we are going backwards. This is how personal development works. Often, the deeper the insight, the greater the challenge and the harder it can actually feel.

The benefit of becoming more self-compassionate in regard to our mental, physical, spiritual and emotional health is well founded and documented. We just need to trust that by keeping our hearts open and having the intention to continue on our path towards a more compassionate frame of mind, we are doing all we can.

This week, how can I keep renewing my intention to be compassionate towards myself and others?

What I think about this reflection:

How I feel about this reflection:

What I will do differently after considering this reflection:

What I am grateful for:

"An important aspect of self-compassion is to be able to empathically hold both parts of ourselves – the self that regrets a past action and the self that took the action in the first place."
Marshall Rosenberg

We are a combination of our genes and our experiences. None of us chose to be born into this society, at this time. These decisions were all made for us. We had no say in the matter.

We developed into the individuals we are today, much of this shaped by the experiences we have had and the genes we inherited. These have made us who we are, given us both our strengths and some areas we wish were more fully formed or adapted for the environment we now find ourselves in. We can still be grateful for who we are and have become despite the challenges we may have faced along the way. We can find compassion and appreciation for all those who have helped us and guided us towards the path we currently find ourselves on. They all did their best with whatever resources they had available. We can accept that we are who we are meant to be and all the benefits that can bring.

As human beings we can learn to accept ourselves. Many of the things that make us respond the way we do in certain situations are instinctive, and we can have little impact rationally or emotionally on how we behave at times. We can feel hurt by one person and then take this out on someone who has done nothing to us.

To cultivate self-compassion we need to get better at understanding ourselves and why we may have behaved in the ways we have. We also need to show ourselves empathy and recognise that, at times, we don't have as much control over our sometimes irrational behaviours as we might like. We can learn to accept and appreciate that we are perfectly flawed.

This week, how can I try to care for all the parts of myself, both the good and the flawed?

What I think about this reflection:

How I feel about this reflection:

What I will do differently after considering this reflection:

What I am grateful for:

"When you are compassionate with yourself, you trust in your soul, which you let guide your life. Your soul knows the geography of your destiny better than you do."
John O'Donohue

Sometimes we have to 'let go' of the outcome and just try our best regardless. We have to trust that we will get to where we are meant to be and will receive from the universe what we need rather than what we want. Even the hard lessons in life are just that, lessons. These help us grow more as people if we can recognise the learning from a situation, often more so than when everything seems to go our way.

By focusing on being and becoming more compassionate towards ourselves, we are more able to trust in ourselves and know that we are exactly where we are meant to be at this point in our lives. This doesn't mean that we don't take responsibility for ourselves or that we sit back and wait for everything to come to us. We still need to act, do all we can to bring about progress and put in the necessary hard work. We know that the greatest rewards can come about when we give something our best shot.

It is often said that 'what will be, will be'. At times, no amount of self-will or desperation to achieve something will take us there. Sometimes we have to accept that maybe it wasn't the right path for us. Often with hindsight we realise that everything happened as it was meant to, and we can become grateful for some of the things that caused us disappointment, purely on the basis that they wouldn't have brought us to the place we are now.

This week, how can I trust in myself and the universe to give me what I need?

What I think about this reflection:

How I feel about this reflection:

What I will do differently after considering this reflection:

What I am grateful for:

Consider your learning about self-compassion over the last four weeks.

Name three things you have learnt about compassion generally:

Name one key thing you have learnt about yourself:

How will what you have learnt benefit you?

What action would you like to take as a result of this learning?

Is there anything you would like to consider further?

"When you are self-compassionate in the face of difficulty, you neither judge yourself harshly, nor feel the need to defensively focus on all your awesome qualities to protect your ego."
Heidi Grant Halvorson

It is natural that when we feel threatened we can act defensively. This can take many forms but is usually directed towards ourselves or others. When we defend ourselves from a place of shame, sadness, hurt or fear by attacking ourselves, and those around us, we can cause immense damage. By trying to accept our feelings for what they are, just feelings, however strong, then we are freed from them to some extent and we are ruling them rather than allowing them to rule us.

At times we might feel the need to build ourselves up to make ourselves feel stronger and more able to face the challenges. This can also be damaging. We think we are deflecting the difficulty, but actually we are avoiding the possibility of feeling what is probably a perfectly reasonable emotion based on the circumstances.

Cultivating self-compassion allows us to recognise, crucially without judgement, that we aren't perfect, that things won't always go our way, and at times life can be cruel and downright unfair. There is nothing wrong here, this is the natural order of things and a brief, but real, moment of self-pity can actually move us towards a place of acceptance for how we feel and allow us to then move on more successfully.

This week, how can I increase my awareness of my emotions and accept them without judgement?

What I think about this reflection:

How I feel about this reflection:

What I will do differently after considering this reflection:

What I am grateful for:

"A moment of self-compassion can change your entire day. A string of such moments can change the course of your life."
Christopher Germer

If we aim to practise one minute of self-compassion each day, or even two lots of thirty seconds, monumental shifts in our lives can start to occur. Just to think kindly towards ourselves, consciously recognise all the good things we have to offer the world and that being who we are is a gift, then we start to feel differently during the rest of the day.

To actively recognise that we are not alone, that there are countless others on a similar journey or at a comparable stage in their lives, really helps us to feel connected to other people, even those we have never even met.

Practising being mindful in the moment, for however short a time this may be, is still practising mindfulness. We start to organically extend this ability the more we actually do it. Habits grow by just doing the same thing over and over again.

Put all these practices together and we find that we are becoming more focused on being self-compassionate than we ever thought possible. We are not chasing false dreams or bowing to idols that will not provide any sense of well-being or happiness for us in the long run. Through the daily practice of self-compassion, we find a deep-seated peace within ourselves and therefore our lives are irreparably changed for the better.

This week, how can I bring about as many moments of mindful self-compassion as possible?

What I think about this reflection:

How I feel about this reflection:

What I will do differently after considering this reflection:

What I am grateful for:

"When we can compassionately see that we fumble, we
make mistakes, or that we are (if only faintly and occasionally!)
aware of the goodness within us that we do not always know how
to express, we start to be aware of feelings of
compassion for ourselves."
Anne Wilson-Schaef

Learning to be compassionate towards ourselves is a process. It is not one that happens overnight. How could it? We have had years and years of not even knowing we needed to be more self-compassionate, let alone actually practising this mindset.

We have very few role models for self-compassion. How many people do we know that show us, in their actions, how much they value themselves? How many of us were brought up in a culture where this was taught and practised? The answer is likely to be very few.

All we need to do, once we recognise that not being so hard on ourselves and cultivating more compassion will help us all lead happier and more fulfilling lives, is take some baby steps in the right direction. Notice our thinking and behaviours without judgement. Recognise how truly interesting we are as human beings for thinking and behaving in the ways we do. Learn to be grateful for these insights and the path we are on towards greater self-compassion.

It would be unthinkable for us to change many years of ingrained behaviour and repetitive thought patterns overnight. Just recognising that we do sometimes get things wrong, but not judging ourselves for this, is a good place to start. We may also start to see the times when we manage to get things right as well.

This week, how can I become more aware of the goodness within me?

What I think about this reflection:

How I feel about this reflection:

What I will do differently after considering this reflection:

What I am grateful for:

"It is unconditional compassion for ourselves that leads naturally to unconditional compassion for others."
Pema Chodron

Often, the compassion we show ourselves and others is dependent on outside factors, receiving care and understanding back, for example, when we find ourselves in need. When we give someone compassion, we might expect their behaviour to change in some way as a result. To let go of the results when we give compassion to others and to expect nothing in return starts with being able to give ourselves the compassion we need. We can support ourselves through our practice of self-compassion and need less from others as a consequence.

To cultivate unconditional compassion for others, we need to let go of the outcome. We need to do the same when we are showing kindness and understanding to ourselves. Even when we are able to respond to our difficulties with understanding and warmth, we may still go on to act in ways that we don't comprehend or foresee. All that is left for us when this situation arises, is to be compassionate towards ourselves. The less we avoid our feelings and accept them as they are, the more we respond to ourselves with comfort and support, the greater the likelihood of a more peaceful, and ultimately happier, existence we create for ourselves. In learning how to persistently do this for ourselves, we become more accepting of other's feelings and journeys and find that we are more able to give others compassion without needing to change the outcome for them. Sometimes, the act of giving compassion to someone is all we can do and, on this basis, it is enough.

This week, how can I show myself and others unconditional compassion?

What I think about this reflection:

How I feel about this reflection:

What I will do differently after considering this reflection:

What I am grateful for:

Consider your learning about self-compassion over the last four weeks.

Name three things you have learnt about compassion generally:

Name one key thing you have learnt about yourself:

How will what you have learnt benefit you?

What action would you like to take as a result of this learning?

Is there anything you would like to consider further?

"The art of peaceful living comes down to living
compassionately and wisely."
Allan Lokos

Bringing more compassion into our lives is a step towards living a life that embraces a peaceful state of mind. This eludes us most of the time, unless we make a conscious decision to try to follow a path which will help us to be more compassionate towards ourselves and others.

This isn't about becoming some sort of guru or spiritual giant. This isn't about telling other people how to live their lives. This isn't about thinking we have it all worked out and nothing will ever hurt or challenge us again. Far from it! In fact, life as we know it will still happen. We will still have to chivvy children along to get them to school on time, make them do their homework and eat food that's good for them. We will still get stuck in traffic. We will still have disagreements with people and feel hurt by other's behaviour. We will still, at times, have to face disappointment and failure. We will still experience loss and grief. Life will still happen.

Going through life with a greater sense of compassion towards ourselves will not stop life happening, but it will help us to cope better with all the challenges and difficulties that will inevitably come our way. When we simply accept our feelings, exactly as they are, with no judgement for ourselves for having them, then we are practising self-compassion. This takes us further down the road of peaceful living than we might have come otherwise.

This week, how can I accept my life as it is right at this moment and feel compassion for myself?

What I think about this reflection:

How I feel about this reflection:

What I will do differently after considering this reflection:

What I am grateful for:

"Be happy in the moment, that's enough. Each moment is
all we need, not more."
Mother Teresa

We live in a society and culture that demands we constantly compete throughout our lives. From an early age we are encouraged to be on our best behaviour at all times, be the top of the class, gain the best exam results, enter the best universities, achieve a glittering career, find and commit to a perfect relationship, have the most perfect children, live in the nicest houses in the best neighbourhoods, drive the latest model of car, wear the best clothes money can buy, have the most active social life and leave the greatest legacy.

To achieve this endless list of requirements as a means of being seen to be successful is, for the most part, exhausting. The emphasis on gain and accomplishment can plague us, drive us to illness and despair because is enough ever really enough? There will always be someone who has achieved more than us and who has managed to reach higher pinnacles of success. Will this competition ever have a winner? Mostly it seems to create losers of us all.

To radically alter our focus to finding happiness in the moment and pursuing activities, work and relationships that engage and sustain us can be life altering. We can discover our true purpose and find deeper meaning than we ever thought possible. Of course, we still have to pay the bills and be involved in things that don't necessarily move us. But if we know that each moment brings us all we need and, connecting with the happiness we may find there, lifts our existence into one of authentic appreciation and true satisfaction.

This week, how can I focus on being happy in the present moment and know this is enough?

What I think about this reflection:

How I feel about this reflection:

What I will do differently after considering this reflection:

What I am grateful for:

"I myself am made entirely of flaws, stitched together
with good intentions."
Augusten Burroughs

There are many amazing aspects to each of us as human beings. There are also any number of flaws in our personalities. Some of these are present because of our genes and experiences beyond our control. These make us who we are, for better and worse, and this is the case for every single one of us. None of us are immune to the laws that make us human.

If we can adapt to viewing ourselves as perfectly flawed human beings, and find acceptance and forgiveness for this fact, we are practising self-compassion. If we recognise how that, for the most part, our intentions are honourable, this can provide the salve for our inevitable imperfections.

Our lack of perfection as human beings is useful to acknowledge. It takes the pressure off us – we aren't meant to be perfect! The ancient Japanese art of Kintsugi repairs cracks in crockery with gold as a means of recognising and cherishing imperfection. The flawed beauty that is present in everything is observed and made all the more valuable and spectacular for it. This art also draws attention to the fact that our scars from life can make us stronger as well as more beautiful.

Our ultimate aim is not perfection – we are all works in progress after all – but acceptance of our whole selves both the good and the flawed. We are all unique individuals and are, mainly, just doing our best regardless of our genes and experiences. The practice of self-compassion allows us to acknowledge that we are good enough exactly as we are.

This week, how can I recognise my good intentions?

What I think about this reflection:

How I feel about this reflection:

What I will do differently after considering this reflection:

What I am grateful for:

"I would like my life to be a statement of love and compassion –
and where it isn't, that's where my work lies."
Ram Dass

None of us ever get everything perfectly right all of the time. That isn't what it means to be human and live in this world. But to aim our focus on love and compassion, in as many of our actions as possible, is a worthy pursuit whether this is directed towards ourselves, in our paid work, in our leisure interests or in our interactions with those around us.

We all have work to do. We never get to a point in life and think we have it all sorted out, we can now quit and rest on our laurels and look at the huge success our life is. We all have areas of our lives that we would like to improve if we are honest with ourselves. We all have aspects of ourselves that would benefit from a more compassionate and loving approach, this is where our work lies.

Being compassionate towards ourselves and others in every waking moment is an impossible feat. We can never achieve perfection in this regard, however, we can make the conscious effort to try our best. To reach the end of our lives and know that we have tried to make a difference by making every effort to value ourselves and others along the way seems like a life well lived and a truly wonderful legacy.

From this week, how can I make my life a statement of love and compassion?

What I think about this reflection:

How I feel about this reflection:

What I will do differently after considering this reflection:

What I am grateful for:

Consider your learning about self-compassion over the last four weeks.

Name three things you have learnt about compassion generally:

Name one key thing you have learnt about yourself:

How will what you have learnt benefit you?

What action would you like to take as a result of this learning?

Is there anything you would like to consider further?

FURTHER RESOURCES

A LIST OF FEELINGS AND EMOTIONS

Six Basic Emotions:

- Happiness
- Sadness
- Anger
- Disgust
- Fear
- Surprise

Full List of Human Emotions:

Acceptance	Affection	Aggression
Ambivalence	Apathy	Boredom
Compassion	Confusion	Contempt
Depression	Doubt	Ecstasy
Empathy	Envy	Embarrassment
Euphoria	Forgiveness	Frustration
Gratitude	Grief	Guilt
Hatred	Hope	Horror
Hostility	Homesickness	Hunger
Hysteria	Interest	Loneliness
Love	Paranoia	Pity
Pleasure	Pride	Rage
Regret	Remorse	Shame
Suffering	Sympathy	

From: Eckman, 2014.

SELF-COMPASSION STATEMENTS

Repeating one of the following statements, silently to ourselves when it feels helpful, allows us to focus on the cultivation and ongoing maintenance of self-compassion:

(Adapted from Neff, 2011)

"This is a moment of suffering.
Suffering is part of life.
May I be kind to myself in this moment.
May I give myself the compassion I need."

"I am finding this really difficult right now.
Everyone feels this way sometimes.
May I hold my pain with kindness.
I am worthy of receiving self-compassion."

"That really hurt.
Anyone could feel this way.
May I be gentle and understanding with myself.
I will try to be as compassionate as possible."

"May I be safe.
May I be peaceful.
May I be kind to myself.
May I accept myself as I am."

"May I accept myself as I am.
I am no different, either better or worse, than anyone else.
I am a human worthy of kindness.
May I find the ways to express my kindness to others."

"May I accept my life as it is.
There are so many people around the world with a life like mine.
There are so many people around the world who would
love a life like mine.
May I be grateful for all the things I have in my life today."

Your Own Self-Compassion Statements:

Include a few words to cover each of the following aspects:

1. Recognise your difficulty/challenge/issue/feeling or emotion.
2. Recognise your shared human response to the above.
3. An expression of your care and concern for yourself in this moment.
4. An expression to recognise your intention to be compassionate to yourself.

Feel free to create your own versions of self-compassion statements that are meaningful to you and note them here:

COMPASSION MEDITATIONS
AND PRACTICES

Short Breathing Meditation for Beginners

You will need about five minutes for this practice to encourage you to be still, focus on your breathing and cultivate mindfulness. Sit or lie down in a comfortable position and take some deep breaths. Close your eyes and smile gently.

Focus gradually on your breath coming in and going out of your body.

Start to count to five, one on each in breath. If your mind wanders don't worry, this is perfectly natural, just bring your attention back to the breath and start counting to five again.

Count to five three times.

On the in breath think of a feeling you would like more of such as love, happiness or peace and focus on this word and the feeling it generates on each in breath. Continue for a minute or so.

Following this, on the out breath, think of a feeling you would like to send out into the world, to the people you care for or for one particular person. This may be love, happiness or peace. Focus on the word and directing the feeling towards the person/people/world for a minute or so. Bring your focus back to the in breath and repeat counting to five, one on each in breath.

Count to five three times.

Take a few deep breaths, and when you are ready open your eyes.

Short Loving Kindness Meditation for Beginners

You will need about five minutes for this practice which encourages you to develop kindness towards yourself. Sit or lie in a comfortable position and take some deep breaths. Close your eyes and smile gently.

Remind yourself that you are bringing your attention to your breath and your experience.

Think of someone who makes you feel happy; allow the feeling of happiness at the thought of this person to enter your heart. Enjoy their presence.

Wish them well – "May you be well, may you be peaceful, may you be safe, may you be happy." Silently repeat three times.

Don't worry if your mind wanders, this is perfectly natural, just gently bring your attention back to the image you have of the person who makes you feel happy.

Now bring yourself into your circle of compassion and wish yourself well. Place your hand on your heart – "May I be well, may I be peaceful, may I be safe, may I be happy." Silently repeat three times.

Take a few deep breaths and enjoy the feeling of peace and happiness in this moment.

When you are ready, open your eyes.

Walking Meditation

You can practice a walking meditation for as long as you like or feels right to you, in any environment.

Try to walk at a steady pace. Focus on your breathing, in and out. Notice the world around you, keep your focus on your breath. You may want to silently acknowledge your immediate environment, without attributing any thought process or judgement at all to what you see, just notice. This assists you to be present in each moment as you walk.

Once you feel you are fully present in the moment, you can turn the focus to your in breath and select a positive feeling or word such as love, peace or happiness to silently say to yourself. You can focus your out breath on another feeling or word that is positive for you.

Repeat these words/feelings on the in and out breaths for a few minutes of walking.

When you are ready, take a few deep breaths and close the practice.

Drawing or Colouring Meditation

There are a number of colouring patterns available in this journal or you can create your own drawings in a sketchbook. You can zentangle or doodle with different coloured pens on a piece of paper – create shapes, lines, blocks of colour, areas free of colour. The point of a drawing or colouring meditation is to provide yourself with an absorbing activity that gives you a break from thinking about other things or acting on those thoughts, albeit for a short period of time. By allowing ourselves to concentrate on a pleasurable and relaxing activity, our minds calm and we are fully engaged in the moment.

One Minute of Self-Compassion

For one minute, you can time this if it helps, think about being kind to yourself. Repeat kind and warm words to yourself, representing feelings that encourage you to feel safe, loved and peaceful. Place your hand on your heart. If your mind wanders, don't worry, this is perfectly natural, just repeat the words again until the minute is complete.

One Minute of Mindfulness

For one minute, you can time this if it helps, focus on this moment. Focus on each second in this minute. Just being here, breathing in and out. Savouring the moment of peace and not doing anything at all, just being, exactly where you are, being you, feeling whatever you do, breathing. Continue until the end of the minute. Don't worry if your mind wanders, this is perfectly natural, just bring your attention gently back to the moment and the breath.

FURTHER READING AND INFORMATION

Neff, K.D. (2011) *Self Compassion: Stop Beating Yourself Up and Leave Insecurity Behind.* William Morrow: New York

Germer, C.K. (2009) *The Mindful Path to Self-compassion: Freeing Yourself from Destructive Thoughts and Emotions.* New York: Guilford Press

Gilbert, P. (2009) *The Compassionate Mind: A New Approach to Life's Challenges.* Oakland, CA: New Harbinger Press

Dalai Lama, XIV. (1995) *The Power of Compassion.* New York: HarperCollins

Thich Nhat Hanh (1991) *The Miracle of Mindfulness.* London: Rider

Armstrong, K. (2011) *Twelve Steps To A Compassionate Life.* GB: Bodley Head

Web Links:

Amanda Super

www.creatingcompassion.com

Kristin Neff

www.self-compassion.org

Centre for Mindful Self-Compassion

www.centerformsc.org

Christopher Germer

www.mindfulselfcompassion.org

Paul Gilbert

www.compassionatemind.co.uk

Paul Eckman

www.listofhumanemotions.com

Acknowledgements

This journal is based on the work of leading worldwide academics in the field of compassion and mindfulness. They are numerous but the author acknowledges the fundamental premise for this book is based on the research and writings of Dr Kristin Neff at the University of Texas. Also, the author would like to acknowledge the work of Dr Christopher Germer of Harvard Medical School and Professor Paul Gilbert at the University of Derby for their ideas, understanding and teachings in the field of self-compassion and mindfulness development. Other authors have also provided inspiration including Brené Brown, Sharon Salzberg, Karen Armstrong, Pema Chodren, His Holiness the Dalai Lama, Jon Kabat-Zinn, M. Scott Peck and Marianne Williamson.

I would like to thank all the people at Matador, particularly Amy Statham and Robert Warner for their expert guidance and assistance in publishing this book.
I would like to thank all my friends and colleagues who commented on the early drafts, especially Jodi O'Dell, for her enthusiasm and ongoing support.
I would like to extend my deepest gratitude to Pauline L.H. and Pauline E. for both showing me the meaning of self-compassion and helping me on my journey.
I would like to offer special thanks to both of my parents.
Finally, I would like to thank my husband, Jonny, for all his support and encouragement as well as his help with the editing process.
I am exceptionally grateful to you all.